THERE I GO AGAIN

To Cari—

WILLIAM DANIELS

There I Go Again | How I Came
to Be Mr. Feeny, John Adams,
Dr. Craig, KITT, and Many Others

William Daniels

Potomac Books

AN IMPRINT OF THE UNIVERSITY OF NEBRASKA PRESS

"The Legacy of 1776" was originally published in March 2016 in New York City Center's *Playbill* and is reprinted courtesy of *Playbill*.

Library of Congress Cataloging-in-Publication Data
Names: Daniels, William, 1927– author.
Title: There I go again: how I came to be Mr. Feeny,
John Adams, Dr. Craig, Kitt, and many others /
William Daniels.
Description: Lincoln: Potomac Books, 2017.
Identifiers: LCCN 2016035738
ISBN 9781612348520 (cloth: alk. paper)
ISBN 9781612349022 (epub)
ISBN 9781612349039 (mobi)
ISBN 9781612349046 (pdf)
Subjects: LCSH: Daniels, William, 1927– |
Actors—United States—Biography.
Classification: LCC PN2287.D27 A3 2017 |
DDC 791.4502/8092 [B]—dc23
LC record available at https://lccn.loc.gov/2016035738

Set in Lyon by Rachel Gould.

For Irene

CONTENTS

ILLUSTRATIONS

PREFACE

Whatever success I've had in my life—and I've had considerable success—has come to me almost accidentally. Granted I developed acting ability and I've worked hard at it. You don't do years and years of eight performances a week on Broadway or on tour or six and seven years of starring roles on television series without working hard. But still, I'm left with the feeling that none of my success was really due to me.

When I'm sent a script to consider, I only see its problems, not its strengths. I have almost always had to be talked into a role, even when the project turned out to be tremendously successful. I've been known to go to the wrong theater to audition for a role I subsequently got—and played for years. Once, while auditioning for a musical, I forgot the lyrics of a song I'd sung for months on Broadway; they hired me anyway. I insisted on having no billing on a series I thought was silly, and that series (*Knight Rider*) ran for years and even after all this time I still get fan mail.

I went "ass backwards" into just about everything—and what a lucky guy I've been.

ACKNOWLEDGMENTS

I wrote this manuscript in longhand on yellow legal pads, so I have to first thank Rachael Lobermann, who spent many hours typing it all up. I have excellent handwriting, but I don't know a damn thing about computers.

Laurie Horowitz took the typed pages and made them resemble something that looked like a book, with paragraphs and everything.

In today's literary landscape getting a publishing deal is difficult to say the least, and so I'm immensely grateful to my literary agents Elizabeth Evans and Laura Biagi with Jean V. Naggar Literary Agency. Elizabeth was the first person interested in shopping the book to publishers, and together with Laura I was introduced to the University of Nebraska Press and the Potomac Books imprint. Acquisitions editor Tom Swanson has been immensely supportive.

Tom's assistant Emily Wendell, along with Jenny Worman and Brian Hamilton, were all very helpful with technical matters.

Jay Matthews had written a wonderful article about the *St. Elsewhere* Emmy night for the *Washington Post*, and so I turned to him and his wife Linda to create a presentation for the publisher (and it was instrumental in selling the book to Potomac).

Finally I'd like to thank Loren Lester, who not only suggested the title but also brought his showbiz knowledge and communication skills to writing and editing the final manuscript.

Note: If I failed to mention my wife, Bonnie, it wouldn't be the first time, but without her this book, and my life as detailed here, would not have been possible.

1

I'd Rather Be Elsewhere

In 1985 I was nominated for a third straight Emmy award for *St. Elsewhere*, the NBC series I did from 1982 to 1988. Having lost twice, I didn't want to go to the Emmy Awards show and lose a third straight time, but there I was with my wife Bonnie, dressed to the hilt, starting out in the limousine but not getting very far. Halfway between the Coldwater Canyon and Laurel Canyon exits on the freeway the limo conked out. The motor went dead—and there we sat.

Since Bonnie's gown was even less conducive to hiking through the Valley heat than my tuxedo, she stayed in the car with the driver and I walked the half mile to the Laurel Canyon exit. As I trudged under the tunnel of the freeway on my way home, a car stopped and a little old lady leaned out the car window.

"Can we drive you?"

There I was in a tux, collar unbuttoned, tie undone, looking like a short Dean Martin coming home from an all-night binge, and two little old ladies (one driving) wanted to take me home.

"Uh, no thank you," I said and continued walking. They slowly followed in the car. She leaned out the window again.

"We know who you are. Are you sure we can't drive you?"

Well, what the hell.

"Okay," I said and got into the backseat. "Take a right. I live just a couple of blocks down."

They dropped me off in front of my house. Out of the monkey suit and on with the TV to watch a McEnroe tennis match.

Not for long. Bonnie was back with a new limo and was standing over me.

"What are you doing?" she asked.

"Watching John play—it's the finals." (I was a big McEnroe fan.)

"Bill," she said, "if we don't go, I am going to be so depressed. I've spent so many times buying a dress for an occasion, getting the makeup on, getting the hair done, getting all fixed up for something, and we don't go, or we walk out, because you're in a snit and I have to go out smiling at everybody, missing everything I was prepared to do. We walked out on the opening night party of *The Graduate*, and we walked out on the film premiere of *1776*." She paused, flustered, and then added, "Goddamnit, I just think you should at least be able to go there and sit through this thing. We're going to Pasadena!"

So I did as she asked, but I was still seething. I got back into the monkey suit, climbed into the new limousine with Bonnie and the same driver, and headed off to Pasadena. Don Johnson was going to win. I knew it. I just knew it. I was certain the studio had sent him a limo that wouldn't break down.

I don't know how long the show had been going on when we arrived. We tip-toed down the aisle and into our row of reserved seats. *Excuse me, sorry, excuse me.*

We had just sat down when I heard, "And the award goes to William Daniels."

Good God! Here we go again back down the row . . . *excuse me, sorry, excuse me* . . . bumping into people's knees, getting out of the row. Someone slapped me on the back—"Congratulations!" Lord, I hadn't prepared anything to say. Oh well. Up on the stage someone handed me the award.

"Thank you, thank you very much." I looked out at the crowd. "You know, I almost didn't make it here." Big laugh.

I went on to tell them how the limo broke down and the two little old ladies, who were probably watching now, rescued me. "Thank you again for the ride," I said.

I was getting laughs, so I figured all wasn't lost. Later that night the press wanted to know if I'd made up the story I'd told in my acceptance speech. What a question. Why would I make up a story like that?

By 1987 I had had a total of five nominations and won twice for my work on *St. Elsewhere*, the famous one-hour series about life in a run-down Boston hospital. *You might be confined here, but you'd rather be "elsewhere."* It was an ensemble show much in the spirit of the game-changing, Emmy-winning series *Hill Street Blues*, which was an ensemble cop show (also from MTM, Grant Tinker's company, which was producing *St. Elsewhere*). And it paved the way for future hit medical dramas such as ER and *Grey's Anatomy*. When *St. Elsewhere* was being developed, I received an offer to play the part of Dr. Mark Craig. An unprecedented five one-hour scripts came with the offer. There was a large cast of characters, an ensemble, with only the occasional appearance, often very brief, of Dr. Craig. When the producer, Bruce Paltrow, called to hear my reaction to the offer, I said that I thought the scripts were wonderful and often very funny but that the part of Dr. Craig was rather small.

"Billy, when the writers see what you do with it they will write for you." And that was exactly what happened—the part got bigger and the storylines got deeper.

In my research for the role I trailed a real-life surgeon at UCLA and even watched him operate on the heart of a small child. He was a great doctor during surgery and a real son of a bitch outside the operating room. The Dr. Craig that the TV audience eventually saw was like this surgeon but also a lot like me. Just ask my wife. I can be rather abrupt, very critical, and sometimes judgmental—a real martinet. As the producers and writers got to know me, they poured all my traits, both positive and negative, into Dr. Craig, who was a great surgeon but not always a nice man. Dr. Craig considered himself the smartest man in the operating room, perhaps the smartest in the entire hospital, and he made no attempt to hide his sense of superiority.

The show had a thirteen-episode order, but it also had a rocky start. We were halfway through filming the first episode when Bruce Paltrow returned from finishing a feature film in London. When he saw the dailies, production came to a halt. The cast was told to take a few days off. Days turned into weeks, and when we were called back we found the director was gone, the cinematographer and camera crew were gone, and several of the actors had been replaced. The sets had been repainted a more drab color, ceilings had been put in to cut down the lighting, and the overall look was of a rather rundown hospital in a lower-class neighborhood of Boston, St. Eligius Hospital, whose façade appeared in the opening shot of the show. Paltrow put together a fine cast of actors, including Ed Flanders and Hollywood legend Norman Lloyd (who as of this writing is still working at the age of 102), along with Ed Begley Jr., Denzel Washington, Howie Mandel, Christina Pickles, Mark Harmon, and David Morse, who all became stars in their own right. During the show's six-year run we also had a roster of guest stars that were the envy of any show before or since: Alfre Woodard, Helen Hunt, Kathy Bates, Tim Robbins, Dorothy McGuire, Betty White, Doris Roberts (who won an Emmy for her role), and Eva Le Gallienne. Real-life couple Steve Allen and Jayne Meadows had Emmy-nominated comedic recurring roles as the hippie parents of Ed Begley Jr.'s character.

And of course, my wife, Bonnie Bartlett, joined the cast in the fourth episode of our first season and remained with us for the entire six seasons of our run, garnering two Emmy Awards along the way.

The casting of Bonnie was rather fortuitous. In one episode, while performing a heart operation, Dr. Craig bragged about how he got his wife to stop smoking; he went out on their front lawn and yelled loudly about her smoking for all the neighborhood to hear and that did it—she stopped. In the next episode, at an awards dinner for "Surgeon of the Year," an honor Craig continually assumed he would win but each year went away empty handed, there sat his wife, who proceeded to light up a cigarette when the doctor left the table for the men's room. At the casting session for the episode, after a number of names were thrown around, Eileen Mack Knight, the casting director at MTM, said, "Why not ask his wife, Bonnie, if she might do it, as a favor?"

The part only had a line or two, and under normal circumstances Bonnie would have turned it down. But the scripts were so well written and we both had such high hopes for this show that she agreed to do it. Now came the hard part—Bonnie didn't smoke! I took her out to the pool house, so as not to stink up our home, and we worked on it. It was a pain in the ass because I'd given up smoking about twenty years earlier, but I taught her how to hit the pack and pull out a cigarette, how to tap it on the back of her hand, how to light up—all of which she got down pat. But inhale—no way! She'd hold the smoke in her mouth and then kind of cough it out.

"Don't cough it out—let it out slowly," I said.

With luck she wouldn't have a coughing spell. The whole preparation of lighting up sold it, and she got the laugh, but you shouldn't look too closely at the actual drag on the cigarette.

The producer and writers must have liked the look of the two of us together because Mrs. Craig became a regular on the show, and she had many wonderful scenes with me and without me for the rest of our run.

For me the role of Dr. Craig was a joy to play. There were so many contradictions in his character—top-notch surgeon and strict disciplinarian in the operating room, yet so foolish in the outside world. Playing such a role over a long run offered a wide range of situations: at one end there was the challenge of facing the loss of a son and at the other the inanity of Dr. Craig's desperately wanting to be named "Surgeon of the Year." I enjoyed the freshness each new story offered, a welcome contrast at the time to the theater, where the same lines are said over and over again.

Led by Tom Fontana and John Masius, the writing was extraordinary for television—or anywhere else for that matter. *St. Elsewhere* succeeded not only because of good writing and a superb ensemble cast but because it always seemed believable to the audience. To capture the frenetic activity of a real hospital the producers relied on a theme song with a throbbing beat that became one of the show's signatures. The music accompanied Dr. Craig and his colleagues in every episode as they strode through the corridors, patient records tucked under their arms, on the way to surgery. *St. Elsewhere* was one of the first TV shows to adopt that walk-fast-and-talk-fast technique, and it was not always easy to pull off. The cameraman had to hold the camera on his shoulder as he was pulled down the hallway on a dolly, shooting the actors behind him. If one person in the crowd of actors made a mistake, we would have to shoot it all over again, and it might take half a day. I personally liked the walk-and-talk scenes; they involved action and took the burden off the script, which otherwise would have to carry the show.

I became fond of Ed Begley Jr., who to this day remains a friend and lives just around the corner from me. Ed's father, Ed Begley Sr., and I had worked together in the days of live television. Ed Jr. and I were the Mutt and Jeff of prime time: he was tall, I was not; he was young, I was middle-aged; he was a hippie, I was the opposite. We often sparred, onscreen and off. Before the cameras rolled, Ed would sometimes drive me crazy because he never learned his lines in advance. I would be ready to film a scene, and he would be over there, learning his lines. He's more of a film actor—a much more improvisational actor than I—and I'm from the theater, so I always knew my lines in advance and he knew he could learn his during rehearsals. I would lay into him occasionally and say, "Any time you're ready, Ed. Is that the way you're going to say it?" And he'd answer, "I'm learning it, Bill. I'm learning it."

The years of filming *St. Elsewhere* at the CBS-Radford Studios in Studio City, about two miles from our home, were happy ones for our family. Both Bonnie and I were able to avoid the horrible traffic jams on LA freeways. We never worked five full days a week. Our scenes sometimes took only an hour or two, rarely more than half a day, and then we went home to our two real-life sons.

Learning lines for an hour-long show isn't easy, especially as you age. Bonnie remembers me sitting out at the pool, day after day, memorizing my lines by saying them aloud. I had to have them down pat because so much of the script was highly technical medical jargon. And on camera I had to make every speech seem like second nature while simultaneously performing heart surgery. The scripts were often very difficult. I knew I was going to be handling surgical instruments that were totally unfamiliar to me, all the while ordering around the other "doctors" in the operating room. So I had to know my lines cold.

Was I convincing as a doctor? Maybe. Several times I've been invited to return to Northwestern University, where Bonnie and I went to college, and to other universities to speak at medical school graduations. I turned down the Northwestern invitation and most others because, after all, I was not a doctor. I had absolutely no insights into medicine that would have impressed anyone with a medical degree. But while I was doing the show I did accept one invitation, to speak at the Salk Institute in La Jolla, the headquarters of Dr. Jonas Salk, who developed the first polio vaccine. When I got up to speak I said something like, "I think Dr. Salk thinks I am a real doctor." I got a big laugh. I don't remember what else I said other than to make a few remarks about all the good work done by Dr. Salk and the March of Dimes to save children's lives.

It was somewhere between the pilot and the first season pickup of *St. Elsewhere* that our producer, Bruce Paltrow, invited the cast of the show to his home for dinner. When I arrived I was greeted by his and Blythe Danner's daughter, Gwyneth. Blythe had played Mrs. Jefferson in the movie *1776* with me ten years earlier, but it was the twelve-year-old Gwyneth who was evidently acting as hostess for the evening.

As I entered, Gwyneth's first words were, "What can I get you to drink?" Amusing, coming from a twelve-year-old, especially since we had never met before, so introductions might have been in order.

"How about a vodka and some ice," I said.

"Regular or producer's size?" she asked.

"Producer's, of course," said I.

What a kid! Lively, precocious, and just as lovely that night as she is today. And Gwyneth has turned out to be as talented as her parents, as the rest of the world now knows. In 1998 she won the Academy Award for Best Actress for her lead role in *Shakespeare in Love*.

St. Elsewhere was actually canceled after the first season, so Bonnie and I took a trip to Europe. When we returned, my son Rob casually said to me, "Hey, I think your show got picked up," and that was the first I'd heard of it. Brandon Tartikoff, the head of NBC programming, was a big fan of the show, and he decided that the show would be allowed to try and find an audience in spite of the terrible ratings. The show never ranked higher than forty-ninth place in the Nielsen ratings, which often determine which shows survive and which die. But over the seasons it attracted a following, especially in the eighteen-to-forty-nine age demographic so important to producers. The critics generally loved us, and our TV colleagues admired us enough that the show won thirteen Emmys for writing and directing, as well as for acting. In 2002 *TV Guide* ranked *St. Elsewhere* number twenty on its "50 Greatest TV Shows of All Time" list.

I won the Emmy in 1985, and the following year both Bonnie and I were nominated for Emmys for *St. Elsewhere*, she for Outstanding Supporting Actress in a Drama Series, I for Outstanding Lead Actor in a Drama Series—and both of us won. That's only the second time, as far as I know, that a husband and wife both won acting Emmys in the same year, for the same show. The first couple to do so was the legendary Alfred Lunt and Lynn Fontanne, who won in 1965 for a made-for-TV movie about Supreme Court justice Oliver Wendell Holmes.

In 1987 Bonnie also won an Emmy for the show. There followed the usual publicity pictures of winners holding their awards. When that was finished, Bonnie and I started to leave, but more photographers stopped us to take pictures of Bonnie.

"Mr. Bartlett, would you please step aside?" one of the photographers said. *Mr. Bartlett!* I stepped aside and the flashbulbs went off. My fifteen minutes of fame were over.

Much to our mutual surprise only writer Tom Fontana offered us congratulations when we won the awards. Not a word from Bruce Paltrow. I think perhaps he had gone into "producer mode," afraid that a compliment would obligate him to give us a raise.

As I said, the days of filming *St. Elsewhere* were happy ones. Because there was such a big cast, I had days off and was able to tool over to Universal Studios (also nearby) to record an episode of *Knight Rider*—the most unusual role I ever had. I was the voice of KITT, a car equipped with artificial intelligence. No one ever saw my face. The dialogue was always between me and David Hasselhoff, the star of the show, and since I wasn't on the set or location when they filmed the scenes, I would give (on tape) three different readings of a line of dialogue so in the editing they could insert the line to fit how David read his line.

I was never on the set. In fact I never met David except at the annual Christmas party. He'd smile and curse me for having it so easy while he was driving the car around in the hot desert and doing stunts. Somehow, when they put David's acting on camera and my recorded voice together, it worked. Go figure.

Sometimes interviewers ask, "Were you proud of *St. Elsewhere?* Was it satisfying work?"

St. Elsewhere definitely made a difference in my life. When strangers recognized me in public they still didn't know my name, but they remembered the uptight doctor on that hospital show. It's an odd way to live, but there are many actors and actresses who have had the same experience: we're not the superstars that the American public can instantly identify. We don't draw big crowds for premieres on Hollywood Boulevard or in Times Square. We don't end up on the cover of *People* magazine. But many of us without name recognition make a fine living, put our kids through college, and, if we're lucky, enjoy long careers precisely because we can play many different kinds of roles. We're not typecast. That's the reason I am still working in my late eighties.

As a character actor I became a star, but a very small one, and I saw time and again how the big stars—the leading men—surrounded by sycophants, lost their sense of reality and then lost everything— their families, their marriages, and, in some cases, their lives.

In a little dressing room just offstage at Radio City Music Hall in New York I was standing in front of a full-length mirror checking out my tuxedo. It was 1986, I had been invited to this Night of a Thousand Stars event to represent *St. Elsewhere*, and at that moment I was not convinced of my place in the starry firmament, to say the least.

I was adjusting my tie when I was elbowed in the ribs, and I was sent staggering away from the mirror. When I turned and looked back, a petite redhead had taken my place and was fussing with her hair. I looked closely: it was Lucille Ball, a real star!

"Oh. You, I like!" she declared. Then she was whisked away. I never saw her again, never knew exactly what she meant. Even though she couldn't remember my name, my guess was that she recognized my face from *St. Elsewhere* or from films or plays or other TV shows I'd appeared in over the years.

I've been a working actor for more than eighty years, and yet when strangers approach me on the street or in the supermarket and say hello, they almost never know my name. Instead they remember my face or maybe a character I played in a TV show or a movie or a Broadway play from years, even decades, before. I tell myself it's better to be recognized than ignored, and it's nice if a stranger, especially an icon like Lucille Ball, says she likes you.

When you think about it, it's a huge compliment for an actor to be remembered for a role he played. It means that, working with the director, the producer, and the writers, I helped create a character, a person utterly different from myself, yet someone real enough to lodge in someone's memory. Memorable characters: that's been the story of my career in show business.

For two years I portrayed America's second president, John Adams, in the Broadway production of 1776, the musical about the hot summer weeks when the Declaration of Independence was written and the American colonies undertook war against Great Britain. Later I starred in the movie version of 1776, still a staple in many high schools, where it's shown in U.S. history classes. In movies, I played Dustin Hoffman's father in *The Graduate* and the ugly American who drove Audrey Hepburn and Albert Finney around France in *Two for the Road*.

People under the age of thirty often remember me as Mr. Feeny, the teacher and principal with a light touch who shepherded a boisterous group of kids through school in the comedy *Boy Meets World*. Part of ABC's Friday-night TV lineup, *Boy Meets World* ran for seven years, from 1993 to 2000, and is still shown in syndication.

I never dreamed of having such a job when I was a kid growing up in Brooklyn. Quite the opposite! I never even thought of a life in show business. That was someone else's dream—my mother's.

2

Life with Mother

I'm sure that everyone, on occasion, thinks of their lives in terms of the mistakes they've made. Looking back, I would say that the first mistake I ever made was as a three-year-old in a brownstone in the East New York section of Brooklyn. The mistake was shuffling my feet with a few hops here and there, but on the beat, to some music that was on the radio. That was all it took to have my mother, Irene, drag me off to the Sonny Hoey Dance Studio.

Sonny, being a practical man, felt it was too soon to be launching this tot's dancing career.

"He can't even count yet," Sonny said.

"I'll teach him to count," replied my mother.

I might have been too young to count, but Sonny wasn't about to turn away a paying customer. And although I didn't learn to count bars of music in time for my first public performance (with full orchestra), at the Brooklyn Lyceum, I did learn to change the step whenever Harry Lefcourt, the orchestra leader, leaned on the crescendo a little and slowed it down. My mother had made me a jockey's riding costume for my debut, so figuratively, as well as literally, I was in the race.

I was born in an apartment in Brooklyn. I don't remember much about the place, but it must have been very modest since the bathroom had no tub or shower. I got my baths in the kitchen sink.

The Great Depression hit in 1929, and that must have been the reason we moved into 47 Hull Street, the three-story brownstone from which I emerged as a three-year-old hoofer. The house was owned by my paternal grandmother, whom we called "Little Gram." (My mother's mother was "Big Gram"). It was one of those brownstones with red stone steps leading up to the main-floor entrance with its double door and foyer. The neighborhood was lower-middle-class blue-collar workers, mostly Irish and German stock, although Italians were beginning to drift into the area. We moved into the basement apartment, and it was from there we made our trips to downtown Brooklyn for our dance lessons.

The Sonny Hoey Dance Studio was around the corner on Broadway in the downtown shopping area of Bushwick. You climbed tin-reinforced steps to the second floor of a dirty-looking building and went through a door with a crinkled-glass partition to Hoey's small office. A separate door led to the dance hall. Mothers sat on long benches along the side wall so they could watch their little adorables blossom into performers. Across from the mothers was the wall of rehearsal mirrors, and at the front end of the room floor-to-ceiling never-been-washed windows overlooked the street.

Down the center of the room, like a red carpet rolled out for royalty, was the gymnasts' mat. And in this place the tumblers and acrobats *were* royalty. Old man Hoey (Sonny's father) had been an acrobat on the vaudeville circuit and was still active, teaching classes in tumbling and operating the bridle that hung from pulleys over the mat. It was a complicated machine with an aura of the guillotine about it. When old man Hoey had some victim strapped into its harness and both came charging down the mat, Hoey running alongside with the pulley ropes in his hand, he looked like some demented driver who's lost control of his buggy and has a runaway horse by the reins, but it was an awesome sight. Frightening. Especially when the victim strapped into that harness was me. Oh, those runs down the mat were terrifying, pulleys and buckles squealing, feet begging to stay on the ground. But no, the crazy old man would yank the ropes and up you flew, eyes popping with fear, forgetting to tuck in your legs, never completing the flip, losing momentum, and finally coming to rest, hanging there motionless, like some hooked fish an angler had walked away from in disgust. I knew in my tiny, terrorized heart that I would never make it into the acrobatic royalty; so did old man Hoey, so did Mother. Tumbling was not for me. Tumbling was for Dolores Leotta, the flying princess, one of

the stars of the studio. To watch her lithe, slim, perfectly propor-
tioned body come whizzing down the mat, starting with the little
hop gymnasts make, into three or four running steps, a "round-off,"
a "flip-flop," another "flip-flop," gaining momentum, and finishing
off with a "back" or a full "twister" was really something. Leotta
hit the ground like the famous Olympian Nadia Comăneci—solid,
perfectly balanced, with a little bounce, arms extended at shoulder level. I watched with a sense of helplessness, without hope, a
mere mortal.

Another kid might have said, "I'm sick" or "I'm scared" or "I
want to go home." But not a peep out of me. I didn't like the place; it
smelled of sweat and was noisy, with the voices of chastising mothers yelling (to be heard over the piano accompaniment) at their awkward little darlings, most of whom had two left feet that they shuffled
three bars behind the music. We were like unwilling draftees in some
midget army, sullenly standing in two or three long lines facing the
mirrors, with Sonny or his wife up front, facing away from us, so we
could ape the correct foot, slowly stumbling through a waltz clog.

"One, two, three, four, five. One, two, three, four, five. Step, step,
kick. Step, step, kick," Sonny's voice would drone on.

Maybe I was learning the steps a little faster than the others, but
so what? As a four-year-old, I didn't like this place. It was too far
from home, from my block where I played, and from my friends who
were important to me, and if they found out what I was doing here
they would laugh and tease me no end. No, they must never know.

I remember that a famous ballet teacher came to Sonny's school
and was impressed by my "natural turnout." He offered to take me
to Manhattan to study, but my parents said no to ballet. It's the only
time I can remember them ever saying no to something involving
show business.

I don't remember being bored with the dancing, but I don't
remember being excited by it either. I suppose some children, maybe
most children, are born to please. *Tap dance? Okay, if that's what you
want. Looky here, I'll jig my feet off. I'm a good boy, I am. Moms love
good boys, right?*

The price for keeping quiet was having to lead two separate lives.

13

A regular schizophrenic. A tap dancer practicing away at night and on weekends and a regular guy at school and with my friends at home. I worked as hard at being just one of the boys on the block as I ever did at dancing. But the dancing came on fast. A "waltz-clog," a "military number," a "soft shoe." The feet just seemed to know where to go. "Light on his feet!" said the pros at Sonny Hoey's. And the dance captain, my mother, was absorbing it all. She never wrote anything down, but she never forgot a step; she just seemed to know how everything should go. She coaxed, needled, and demanded, but she never flattered. And when we hurried home from those Saturday lessons, I'd show the new steps to my sister, Jackie.

"No, two slap steps, then the break, and then the double wings," my mother would say. So we had two lessons for the price of one, and we also had a team.

My sister Jacqueline (later, she dropped the *e*) was two years younger than I was. She had big eyes in a round, freckled face, a big smile, a throaty voice, and a raucous laugh. She also cried at the drop of a hat. She'd follow someone she liked to the ends of the earth. Usually me, her big brother. At this time in our lives she seemed to follow me everywhere, and when she didn't she was getting into mischief. But you had to love Jackie, everyone did, and I spent a lot of time stemming her tears by giving her a ride on the "penny ambulance," which was simply taking her by the shoulders from behind and running her around the place, with me yelling *ding a ling a ling* like an idiot. That always delighted her. The expression in those days was that Jackie had "a lot of personality," a judgment solemnly meted out by friends and neighbors who had quickly gotten the picture that these kids were going into show business. They could see the lights in my mother's eyes, and they spelled *Jackie and Billy Daniels* up on a marquee.

By now Jackie and I were doing tap routines together. From the beginning Jackie always had a breezy, devil-may-care approach to dancing. She was always the best singer, with that big throaty tone, but her dancing was a bit slapdash. If she messed up a step or two, she'd just smile harder and keep plugging away. No one seemed to notice, except me. I learned never to try and get in sync with her;

she always found her way back. She was the star of the team. She got all the "oohs" and "ahhs," some of the laughs, and always the most applause. Once we were dancing together, we were "an act," and Mother didn't hesitate to show us off anywhere—at an aunt's or a cousin's or after coffee and cake at a friend's house. The rug would be pushed back and we were asked, begged, cajoled, and finally ordered to perform. To the accompaniment of my mother's unique brand of humming-singing and a *da ta, da tat a, da*, off we'd go, jigging away, giving the folks our latest routine. Maybe if I'd been in sneakers it would have put a stop to it. But no, there I was in freshly pressed pants, Buster Brown collared shirt, and shiny, hard-soled shoes. I was ready to go. What little resistance I made was pointless. My mother, Irene, was very insistent, and she was very proud of us. She put her whole heart and soul into every show we did, no matter who it was for or where we had to do it. The payoff for all her work was the performance. Irene knew it all by heart, all the words of the songs. All the arrangements were hers, and so were the big endings. It was all hers—the song, the dance steps, the finale, the kids. And she bathed in the glory. Yes, we were a team now—the *three* of us.

Irene must have scanned the daily papers for any items about show business. That was where she had found the Sonny Hoey Dance Studio, and it was in the *New York Daily Mirror* where she spotted something about the *Nick Kenny Children's Show*. It was a fifteen-minute variety show featuring children performing on radio station WMCA. Every month or so they auditioned for new talent at the station. Well, off we went one evening with Irene to Fifty-Second Street and Broadway, where the second-floor studio was located. The auditions were run by Charles Kenny, Nick's brother, and we soon stood in front of him and started our tap routine. We hadn't gotten very far into it when Charles Kenny, in a loud voice, said, "No. No, not tap dancing. This is radio!" We stopped and looked at Mom. Mr. Kenny turned to Irene and said, "Now if they could sing . . ."

So home we went. Irene taught us a song and dragged us back to the next audition. We sang.

"No, no," said Kenny. "Not in unison, in harmony!" Irene dragged us back home and taught us the harmony. Back we went for the third time. We sang. "That's it," said Kenny. And Irene's face lit up in a smile.

Our first performance on live radio came soon after. It was in one of WMCA's studios, and there were maybe forty or fifty people in the audience, mostly friends and families of the children. In front was a small stage with steps on either end. On stage right sat a man at the piano, and there was a microphone at center stage. For our debut performance Irene had taught us a lovely Irish song entitled "I'll Take You Home Again, Kathleen." When it was our turn, we crossed to the microphone and I looked out to the audience. There was Irene, standing in the back of the house. I knew I would be doing this for her. The opening lines of "Kathleen" can be tricky. The melody line rises and the harmony line crosses over into a lower register, and I got off on the wrong foot, losing the harmony line. At that, Irene walked down the side aisle, up the steps, and onto the stage. She stood next to me and sang the correct harmony until I got back on it. Then she left the stage, walked to the back of the house, turned, and listened to us complete the song.

Years later, when I was working with Jerome Robbins on the iconic musical *Gypsy*, I would remember this moment.

Nick Kenny not only ran his radio show, but he took his little troupers on what in those days were called "benefits." They took place just about anywhere: an Elks Club lodge, a Knights of Columbus council, a political rally, a hospital for veterans of World War I—this was the scariest of all, as men with body parts missing pushed up in their wheelchairs to within ten feet of where you were performing; you didn't know where to look. In retrospect it was a nightmare, but as a child I did what was expected of me. Over the course of four or five years we did more than a hundred of these benefits, and we weren't paid a dime. Irene's mantra was that we were gaining experience. Maybe she was right. I learned much later that the Kenny brothers were paid for each and every one of those benefits.

These experiences subconsciously played a part in my becoming insistent on the "money factor"—most of my life I wouldn't accept a role unless I was made aware of how much I was being paid. Being taken advantage of as a child performer no doubt also played a part in my work as president of the Screen Actors Guild, when I was called on to stand up for commercial actors who were seriously underpaid.

It's important to note that my parents never made any money off their kids either. They both had day jobs—my father was a brick-layer and my mother was a telephone operator. I have memories of my mother working all day and then coming home and sewing costumes all night. My mother was very good at her telephone job and continued to do that kind of work almost until the day she died.

One of the "freebies" my sister and I performed was at a political gathering for Al Smith, then governor of New York. There was a huge auditorium, a small orchestra, and hundreds of people. Jackie and I were to do one of our song-and-dance numbers. Walter Winchell was known to provide some headliner stars for these big events. He persuaded or coerced them into appearing for fear of bad press in Winchell's popular column in the tabloid *Daily Mirror*. On this occasion he was able to provide Eddie Cantor, a very big star. Mr. Cantor appeared backstage in a state of great agitation. In a very loud voice I heard him say, "What am I doing here? I don't have my accompanist. What do they expect me to do?" Jackie, age seven, and I, age nine, stood in the wings waiting to go on, listening to all this. And I thought to myself, *If he's scared, what about me?* It was the first time since I was four that I had said those words to myself. Jackie must have been frightened, too. Years later, when I voiced these impressions, Eddie Cantor's daughter informed me in the nicest, kindest way, that her dad never went onstage scared; she was probably right. But as a child, I took his agitation to be fear.

He went on right ahead of us and was greeted with tumultuous applause. He stopped, he smiled, and he began to sing, hat crushed to his chest. We had to wait quite a while before we got to go on. But whether it was fear or anger that I saw in Eddie Cantor that night, I have learned over the years that most talented performers and actors experience fear (let's call it nerves), before they go onstage. I'm told Laurence Olivier would peer at the audience through the peephole in the curtain and curse them before going on to perform.

Kim Stanley would sometimes throw up in her dressing room before going onstage. The more talented they were, the more demands they appeared to make upon themselves.

By the time I was nine I considered myself a pretty good tap dancer, and while watching movies—we went every now and then, not often—I found my hero.

Shirley Temple was a big star in those days and about the same age as Jackie. In one of Temple's films, *The Little Colonel*, she had this lovely tap dance routine with a tall, elegant black man who smiled at her with seemingly genuine warmth as they danced. She, looking up at him, smiled not quite so genuinely (probably because she'd been told to keep smiling), but it was his movement that drew me in; I couldn't take my eyes off him. His dancing looked so effortless and graceful; he seemed to glide across the screen. And his taps—clean and precise. Shirley Temple was undoubtedly a talented little girl, but oh, she was lucky to have such a partner as Bill "Bojangles" Robinson!

The only fan letter I've ever written in my life was to "Bojangles" Robinson. I don't know where my mother sent it, but believe it or not I received a handwritten reply on the stationery of the Book Cadillac Hotel in Detroit. He thanked me for my letter and said I must keep dancing, practicing, working hard, and one day, he was sure, I would find my name up in lights. At the end of the letter he invited me and my parents to come as his guests to his next engagement at the Cotton Club in midtown Manhattan (the original Cotton Club was in Harlem). He even gave us the date on which we should be there.

The Cotton Club was on Fifty-Second or Fifty-Third Street between Seventh Avenue and Broadway, upstairs in a two-story building. When we gave our names at the door (just Irene and I; Dad stayed home with Jackie), we were led to a ringside table in an enormous room with a raised stage—what we today call a thrust stage—with tables covered in white tablecloths surrounding it on three sides. People sat dining, eating, and drinking in this supper club, and a waiter came to our table, asked us what we'd like to drink, and handed us menus. I looked at Irene, and she looked at the menu and said, "Two ginger ales, please." She closed the menu and didn't look at it again.

The show had already started as we sat down; Cab Calloway—the "Hi-De-Ho" man—and his orchestra were going full blast. He stood in front of the orchestra in a suit of white tails waving his baton wildly while a group of beautiful black women in tiny costumes danced in front of him. I looked around and saw I was the only kid in the audience. Irene studied the dancers, without expression, as if she were memorizing the routines; I don't know if she approved of the whole thing or not, but those girls certainly held my attention.

After the chorus line left, a lady singer took the stage, and after she sang Mr. Calloway said, "Ladies and gentlemen, it gives me great pleasure to present the great Mr. Bill Robinson!" And there he was—the man I saw in the movie, the man who had invited us to the Cotton Club. He shook hands with Mr. Calloway, went to center stage, said a few words to the audience, and then started to softly tap, without the orchestra, smooth, with arms extended, fingers moving like he was playing a piano as the orchestra came in softly behind him in what you'd call a vamp. I listened to taps I'd never heard before. His act must have lasted a half hour, maybe longer. Between numbers he ad-libbed with Calloway, and then when he finished his set he walked over to the edge of the stage, where I sat, my head barely above the stage floor, bent down, held out his hand, and shook mine, saying, "This is for you." And he began his famous slap step, one leg out at a time, forming little circles with the toe of each shoe and making taps with that foot that were as rapid as machine-gun fire, *rat a tat a tat a rat a ta*, first one foot then the other, his upper body absolutely still. I tried to teach myself that step for years; it requires a completely relaxed leg, the effort going only to the foot. It's what in athletic circles is called "relaxed effort." He did that step all the way off the stage and exited! Now tell me, here is a man, a big star, who receives a fan letter from a little eight-year-old kid and sits down and takes pen to paper and not only answers him with encouragement but invites him and his mom to the Cotton Club as his guests to see him perform. Can you imagine anyone of his prominence doing that today? What a man! Mr. Bojangles!

When it was over, Irene asked for a check (we'd had just the two ginger ales each), and the waiter said, "There's no check ma'am, you're Mr. Robinson's guests."

Oh my God, I thought. *I could have had a hamburger and french fries.*

While scanning the daily newspapers Irene came across *The Horn & Hardart Children's Hour*. Alice Clements was a partner with her husband, Ike, in a Philadelphia-based public relations firm that represented the Horn & Hardart chain of "automats," or self-serve restaurants. They consisted of walls filled with little windowed boxes that you could look into. Each box contained something to eat— sandwiches, desserts, and so on. You put your coins in the slot, opened the little door, and got the food of your choice. An invisible worker behind the wall would then refill the box for the next paying customer. We ate there every Sunday after the show, Irene networking with the producer.

I hated it. For some reason I felt it was low class. Any bum with a couple of nickels or dimes could come in and buy a piece of pie, sit down right next to you, and eat it. This class consciousness was odd, especially since I was a just a kid from lower, lower East New York, Brooklyn. Where did I even get such a concept? I thought I was too good for the place, but I might have also wanted to get away from Alice Clements and *The Horn & Hardart Children's Hour*.

Ms. Clements started producing her radio show in Philadelphia, and after it was successful she took it to network radio in New York. We auditioned for the show in New York and were chosen to be a part of their permanent company of performers: me, Jackie, and now our baby sister, Carol. Carol started in the business when she was just three years old. She was so young that often she could be found crawling under the piano at our Saturday rehearsals for the Sunday morning show. And because that was where we would find her, Ms. Clements nicknamed her "Termite."

This is how the rehearsal would go: you sat with all the other children (there were quite a few since this was an hour show) and waited your turn to go to the piano, where Ms. Clements, the producer, and Morty Rappé, the pianist, stood. Ms. Clements preferred to be called Aunt Alice (as if we were all a big family, except she was the only one making any money). When your turn came you went to the piano and handed Morty your music. He scanned the pages briefly, struck up a music introduction, and off you went singing some non-sensical number like "I Dug a Ditch in Wichita" or "The Hawaiian War Chant." If you had trouble with the song, Aunt Alice would say, "Take it from the top again." She never criticized and always com-plimented, but if you got ten minutes of rehearsal you were lucky.

Jackie and I were probably eight and ten years old, respectively. When Carol came along, this is how our routine would go: Jackie would sing the melody; I sang the harmony. We learned a new song every week for years. We'd do a chorus of the song and then sing, "Now our three-year-old sister has something to say—tune totin' Termite, take it away!" (composer credit to Irene Daniels). And on Carol would come with a strong, husky voice that belied her years; she was gorgeous, by the way, a young Vivien Leigh. She'd sing her chorus, then we'd end with us doing another thirty-six bars and out.

Again, no money—just, as Irene used to say, *experience*. We did this show for years. I continued to do it even later, when I was act-ing in *Life with Father* (1945–47). When the radio show became one of the earliest television shows, broadcast one hour live on the NBC network every Sunday morning at ten, we went with it.

Television was in its infancy—the TV network wasn't even sure of its own technology. Jackie and I were asked to come down to Rockefeller Center to an experimental studio—3H—that was filled with blindingly hot overhead lights; the only way that they could get the shows to record at that time was if they were bathed in light. The studio was so hot that I couldn't even touch the microphone. My sister and I sang a song once through and got out of there as quickly as we could.

Eventually NBC figured out how to do it right, and so we spent our weekends on the third floor of the NBC studios, rehearsing and then performing in Studio 3A, where years later I would perform as an actor in such shows as *The Philco Playhouse*, *Somerset Maugham Presents*, and *The Robert Montgomery Show*.

There were a few teenagers in our company, but most of us were much younger, and you could find the children running around the third floor outside Studio 3A making up games, burning off energy (warding off nerves?). Most kids had schoolyards to play in, but we had the corridor outside of Studio 3A. And I also had my other playground in the NBC building—the ninth floor, where I could stand at a railing and look down on Studio 8H, where the conductor Arturo Toscanini would receive the undivided attention of the NBC Symphony Orchestra. I didn't know much about classical music yet, but I enjoyed those moments, watching the precise, simple movements of the maestro.

This was live television, not tape; you made a mistake, and it went out to the world. I can remember, more than once, the show already on the air and me pounding on the door of the ladies' restroom to get my sister out of there. *Jackie, we're almost on!* Was she being ornery? I don't think so; I think she was nervous, maybe even frightened half to death.

We took this tension home with us. To the dinner table, or to the piano in the living room rehearsing for the weekly performance. If there had been a mistake, a flubbed line, or a missed cue in the last performance, it was treated like there had been a death in the family. Sometimes there was complete silence going home in the car from the studio. Once Irene was sitting in the front seat while my father was driving us over the Queensboro Bridge, and she suddenly sang out a phrase we had missed. We had embarrassed her and were supposed to be embarrassed as well. Turning to my father she said, "Was that so hard?" More silence. And then, "Sing it," she said. So Jackie and I sang it correctly this time, followed by more silence.

Ironically, at the end of *The Horn & Hardart Children's Hour* TV shows, the cast of children would gather around the microphone and sing our closing number. It went like this:

Less work for Mother
Just lend her a hand
Less work for Mother
And she'll understand
She's our greatest treasure

Just make her life a pleasure
Less work for Mother now

Actors make mistakes, flub lines, but to this day, whenever I do, I'm terribly embarrassed. Years later, in the out-of-town try-out of *1776* in Washington, I was given some changes in the lyrics of a song in the afternoon rehearsal, and at that evening's performance I messed them up. Back in my dressing room I had to go into the toilet and close the door because I had broken down in tears. I don't know how to describe it, but there's such a sense of humiliation. Shortly after, the director and producer came in. They saw that I was upset. They shrugged and laughed it off. Of course they weren't the ones who had to face that audience during those terrible moments of getting back on script.

As I look back on my career as a child performer I don't remember ever saying no, but I realize that I did find a way to gain some respite. I needed to be left alone, to be temporarily free of familial obligation. So I got sick. I mean really sick. Between the ages of five and eleven I had acute pneumonia four times. I can remember sitting in a movie house, knowing I was sick, waiting until I had chills and sweating and thinking, *Now I'm really sick*, before going home, where Irene found my temperature to be 103 degrees. One time I was delirious, seeing the curtains in the bedroom come alive and take different shapes. This was before penicillin, so a serum had to be put together and tested before it was given to me.

I wound up in the hospital twice. Ah, pure heaven! I had candies on the stand next to my bed, which I offered to the nurses to gain their attention. And the alcohol rubs they gave me were cool, soft, and caressing. The pneumonia left me with a permanent bronchiectasis, but who cared? Those hospital stays were some of my happiest childhood memories.

Another time I landed in the hospital is not such a happy memory. When I was about seven my father took me into the shower and examined my penis—I had no idea what he was doing and he never explained it. He then declared that I had an "infection," and the next thing I knew I was waking up in a hospital bed with a bandage on my genitals. Traumatized, I thought for sure they had cut off my penis. Years later I figured out that it was a circumcision, but at the time—not a word of explanation from my parents. I had been taught to follow instructions and not ask questions. Not even in a case like that.

There were a few other respites from performing that I fondly remember. One was when we were invited to Big Gram's house in Bay Ridge for Sunday dinner. My grandmother's first husband, Jack Bulger, had left her and her young daughters. Jack was from a well-to-do family—a family who felt he had married beneath him when he married my grandmother Kate. Jack moved around the fringes of show business and was at one time a manager of Mickey Walker, a middleweight boxing champion. I know my mother idolized Jack, and she probably got her show business ambitions from imagining what his life was like. When he died, Jack's sister wouldn't allow Kate and her two daughters, Irene and May, into Jack's wake until Kate agreed not to mention that she was his former wife and that the girls were his daughters.

When Jack left the family, Kate, alone and with two young daughters to raise, went to work in the restaurant at the St. George Hotel in Brooklyn. I was told she made salads. It was there she met Anthony Jaccarino, a racetrack bookie who worked for a gambling syndicate.

They married and moved into a big house in Bay Ridge, and Kate spent the rest of her life praying for forgiveness for having married twice (without getting a divorce)—a sin in the Catholic faith and illegal as well.

Anthony Jaccarino was known in betting circles as "Jack Tan," a name that in those days smacked of the Mafia, but I never learned of any connections. My father never warmed to Jack Tan. I, on the other hand, adored him; he was the only grandfather I'd ever known. He walked around with a big roll of bills in his pocket, and when he met a bettor with a winning slip, he would take out the money and pay him off right there on the street. I remember once standing by his desk in the living room while he sorted out his slips and payoffs. He always talked gruffly to me, though he never meant it. "Whadda ya want? Get outta here," he'd say, and I would stand my ground.

Finally he'd say, "Here—scram," and he'd hand me a twenty-dollar bill. "Take a cab home." Once, on our way to the trolley to go home, I raised my hand and hailed a taxi. It stopped, and my folks were too embarrassed to send it away. We drove home with my folks giving me dagger looks, because they needed that twenty.

We all called Kate "Big Gram," though she was only five feet tall and almost as wide. She cooked a huge Sunday dinner, with her husband supervising. He'd occasionally walk into the kitchen, taste the tomato sauce, stir the soup, and walk out. Dinner took all afternoon and into the early evening. We were served soup, then salad, then pasta, and then a roast or chicken with vegetables, ending with fruit and cheese and sometimes a sweet pastry—a cannoli or fruit tart that Jack had brought home. He shopped for a lot of the food himself, and I'd sometimes go with him. He tasted everything before he bought it—the cheese, the salami, all the Italian ingredients—and I'd get to taste it, too.

When I was seven or eight years old my grandfather took me and Big Gram to Saratoga for the racing season. It was the middle of the Depression and the town was wide open, with gambling everywhere. We walked down the street, and Jack stopped at a group of men playing craps right on the sidewalk. He watched a minute and then laid down a twenty-dollar bill while some guy threw the dice. Then my grandfather picked up his twenty and someone else's twenty and walked away. We walked on and he said, "Here, buy yourself a pair of shoes," and handed me one of the twenties, and I thought, *Boy, this is a great way to make money.*

He took me to the racetrack, where his syndicate had a betting booth. This was before pari-mutuels; betting was legal, and those betting booths ranged all along an outdoor aisle right next to the racetrack. The odds on each race varied from booth to booth, and a bettor could shop for the best odds before making his bet.

"You wanna see the horses?" my grandfather asked. He took me to a railed circle where the horses with riders were being walked around. "You wanna bet on a horse? Here." He handed me three dollars. "Pick a horse." I picked a white horse mostly because it was all white. "Don't pick that one, pick the brown one."

"I want the white one," I whined.

"All right, pick the white one."

The white horse ran last and the brown one won.

"You see, it's always better to take the other guy's bet than to bet yourself," he said. Jack Tan's words of wisdom.

In 1939 the World's Fair in Flushing Meadows must have contained many buildings and exhibitions that predicted what the future might look like. I never saw those intimations of the future; I was stuck in the present in the Gas Exhibit, where Jackie and I did a fifteen-minute radio show each week. In fact I never even got to look around the Gas Exhibit; we were whisked in to stand at a microphone while an announcer introduced us: "The Daniels Family!" We sang two or three numbers and were whisked out. I remember wanting to see the heavily advertised "Billy Rose's Aquacade," with all those young ladies in bathing suits, but that never happened either. I can't remember who sponsored this little radio show or whether we were paid, but if we were paid, I wouldn't have seen any of it anyway—too young. But I wasn't too young later, during the almost three years I worked in *Life with Father*. My salary there ranged from $57.50 a week to finally $75 a week (no small change in the 1940s). But I never saw any of that either; it went into the family kitty. I was given $10 a week allowance; I guess that's all Irene thought I needed.

Many decades later, when I started writing this book, I started seeing a psychologist, Dr. Estelle Shane, who suggested that I was an abused child. I was shocked to hear such a description—that I had been robbed of a normal childhood, forced to perform, and put into situations that I had no control over. It was unhealthy, my doctor said, that I was unable to express my anger, my fears, and my dread of knowing what was expected of me in the future. Also hurtful was my mother's failure to say "good job" or "well done," compliments surely all children need to hear. Mother believed, rather firmly, that children might get "swelled heads" if they had too much praise.

It has taken me a long time to agree with this diagnosis. It is true that my sisters and I were the tools of my mother's ambitions—her ambitions not just for her children, but for herself. I'm still in love with my mother, as are most men who are willing to admit it—though she died almost three decades ago.

However, I think occasionally about all those evenings when my sisters and I were performing when we should have been home in bed. Everything took a backseat to our performances, even education. When we were performing, we didn't get home until midnight or even later. Then we were up at 8:00 a.m. to go to school. I must have been exhausted, but I was like a robot, doing exactly what I was supposed to do. Sometimes kids can suffer without even knowing they are suffering.

My theory is that Irene, as a young woman, never had the courage to try show business on her own. She also didn't have the right circumstances; her family was very poor. There had been no opportunity for her to do anything adventurous even if she had wanted to, and I'm not sure she really wanted to. So she transferred all that pent-up ambition to her kids, though always in a loving manner. She didn't mean to be cruel if she was. Cruel is the wrong word—determined, demanding, but never physically abusive. She simply had her eye on the prize—her kids, whom she felt sure had a career in show business.

Now that I'm older I realize that my mother had great social skills that eased my way into the business. She could get along with everybody. She had friends everywhere, some famous, many not. She became very close to the people who ran *The Horn & Hardart Children's Hour*. We went out to Philadelphia to visit them. And much later she was a wonderful grandma to our two sons.

But there was a lot I missed as a child because I was always working. I rarely got to play in the streets with my friends. On one of the few occasions when I told my parents that I'd like a chance to be a regular kid doing regular things, it was because I wanted to play football. The games were on the weekend, and we were always booked.

Then one day my parents put my football gear in the car. After we performed we drove to Queens, where my friends were playing. I did a quick change in the car. We parked on the edge of the field and I ran out. I hadn't played with these guys or even practiced with them, but somehow I was allowed to join the game. I had missed most of it, but then I missed most of everything in those days. The football game was a one-time event, a gesture my parents made at giving me a shot at childhood.

I wonder what in the 1930s brought on the public's love of listening to or watching children's entertainment such as *Nick Kenny Children's Show* or *The Horn & Hardart Children's Hour* or *Coast to Coast on a Bus* and *Let's Pretend*. And all those benefits we did! Was it because it was cheap entertainment? I remember taking my parents aside and making that accusation when I was an adult.

"There we were," I said, "up there on the stage, too young to know how nervous and frightened we were, singing and dancing in front of an audience of strangers while you stood back with the rest of the parents, enjoying yourselves, having a night out. It was cheaper than going to the movies, wasn't it?"

My father looked away, and there were tears in my mother's eyes. But they said nothing.

Now, I think they could have—and should have—reminded me of our dire financial straits during the Depression and how they hoped for something better for their children—and why they thought that a future in show business might be the answer.

My mother was really the ultimate stage mother, and my father did nothing to stop her. But show business was no more precarious and uncertain than the lives we actually led in the 1930s and 1940s, and in retrospect my parents were right. At least when it came to me.

3

Life with Father

Up to this point you may have noticed that I haven't said much about my father. It's difficult for me to write about him. Childhood impressions never leave you, and we were children during the most unhappy and difficult part of his life. He had an unfortunate childhood. His father died when he was a teenager, and he was his mother's least favorite of her three sons, even though I know he was the brightest. He was offered a scholarship to a highly regarded technical high school, Cooper Union, in Manhattan, but still couldn't afford to go and was sent out to work when he was fourteen. An uncle took him to the basement of my grandmother's house and taught him how to lay brick. My father spent the rest of his working life laying brick and hating it.

My parents married when they were sixteen years old. Were they ill suited for each other? I'm not sure. They had horrific fights throughout my childhood. Every evening meal would end in a fight. I often left the table with stomach cramps and lay on the couch with a pillow under my stomach. Also, my sister Jackie was always aggravating my dad. I became the arbiter. I think it made me old beyond my years. These things stay with you, and they colored my relationship with my father no matter how hard I tried to change it.

We lived through the Great Depression. Jobs were scarce, and when it rained or snowed bricklayers couldn't get work. Money was always a worry at our house. My mother even on occasion had to go to the police station for milk that was being given out for kids. I think my father was a good man who was angry and frustrated by the cards he was dealt. Had he been given the opportunity, he would have excelled at any engineering job. He was a top-notch bricklayer, always in demand when there was work to be had. He thought nothing of working all day, coming home, and then driving us to Manhattan after dinner for one of the many benefits we performed. But first he had to shower. Every day after work he would be in that shower for what seemed like hours, scrubbing off all the dirt and cement that he hated.

He'd drive us home from our performance, usually after midnight, even though he had to get up the next morning early enough to be on the job at eight. He never complained about this routine. Looking back, I realize that seeing us kids make it in show business was not just my mother's ambition but my father's as well.

When I was starring in *1776* on Broadway in 1970 but living in Connecticut during the summer, my father would drive me to the theater every night and then take me home after the final curtain. What he did in between I don't know, but it was a long wait. He clearly loved doing it, and I think it was simply a chance for him to share, in a small way, in his son's success.

I was never close to him—nor was he to me. And that bothers me now. We never did the things that fathers and sons do together—play ball, go to a game, see a movie. There was never any time for that. He never tried to teach me anything or give me advice—not once. But there was one thing that he did do for me. From the *Journal American* newspaper he would cut coupons you could use to get free books. He stacked the coupons up (there were piles of them), and when he had finally collected enough he got me a cheap edition of the complete works of Mark Twain and Charles Dickens. He realized that I liked to read, so he did that for me.

Later, when my father was an old man, he spent a lot of time with us—he loved the house and garden in Santa Barbara and going to a restaurant called Pane Vino, where he enjoyed making conversation with the Italian waiters.

But I often racked my brains for something to say to him. I took him to the library and picked out mysteries for him to read.

I took him for what he called "coffee and . . ." We would sit there having coffee, trying desperately to make conversation, but by then we were really strangers. I had somehow left him way behind, and to this day I feel guilty about it. He lived about twelve years longer than my mother and died on September 11, 2001, early in the morning, and never knew that the Twin Towers had come down.

When I became a successful actor, my father was terribly proud of me—but the distance between us remained. And oh, how I wish it had been different.

It was at the beginning of the school year, the sixth grade, at St. Clement's Catholic School in South Ozone Park in Queens (we had moved "up") when the teacher, the Dominican nun Sister Dorothy Marie, had us all standing at our desks and singing some popular song while she searched for candidates for the church choir. She walked up and down the schoolroom aisles listening to the children's voices. Suddenly she stopped and looked around as though she'd heard something she hadn't expected. Weaving her way through the aisles, she stopped at my desk. She listened for a moment and then said, "You're singing harmony!" Actually, for me, it was what I always sang; my sister Jackie took the melody. And so I found myself in the church choir and at the beginning of a special relationship with Sister Dorothy Marie and her close friend, Sister Joan Therese.

They soon learned that I was a song-and-dance man with my sister and that I performed two or three nights a week. They must have realized that I was up rather late on those nights, often not getting to bed until midnight or 1:00 a.m. I think they gave me a certain amount of leeway when it came to my schoolwork and my homework, which at times must have been pretty slapdash.

Sister Dorothy Marie loved her music and her choir, and as I approached graduation she made me aware of a high school, rather far from where we were then living. It was called the High School of Music and Art, located at 135th Street and Convent Avenue, right across the street from City College in upper Manhattan. The sisters urged me to apply. I auditioned as a voice student and was accepted.

By then we had moved to Valley Stream on Long Island. I was out of the district and so I couldn't legally go to the High School of Music and Art, but the two nuns let me use their address (and no one was the wiser).

Thus began one of the busiest and most joyful periods of my life.

Busy because I had an hour-and-fifteen-minute bus and subway ride to school (even if I had been up late performing the previous night) and then a long walk up Morningside Heights to get to class at 8:30 a.m. I often fell asleep on the subway, but I never missed my stop!

It was the early forties—at least a decade before Dr. Martin Luther King Jr.'s emergence as a national figure. The civil rights movement wasn't yet apparent to many Americans, but racial tension certainly was. I don't remember many black students at the High School of Music and Art even though it was surrounded by Harlem. It was my first encounter with the pernicious system known as racial segregation. And it wouldn't be the last.

It was a long slope of a walk from the subway stop up to Morningside Heights, and at each level of the climb there was a policeman, presumably to guard the white children as they arrived at school in the morning. They were there again when the students left in the afternoon. There were no outdoor activities after school. You were expected to go right up to school and then right back to the subway to go home.

One day I made the mistake of going to a bus stop on the street in back of the school, across from which was a concrete wall that surrounded CCNY's athletic field. I was going to take a downtown bus to visit a fellow student's piano lesson in one of the apartments above Carnegie Hall (I dreamed of learning to play the piano). There were some black students getting out of school and they walked right by me, but they focused on a pudgy kid from my school who was also waiting for the bus. When I noticed them gathering at the end of the block, I immediately sensed trouble. The group of boys was now growing (one new arrival was a girl), and they sent the smallest kid down to confront my pudgy schoolmate.

"Did you call me a n—?" the small kid said.

And before the petrified pudgy kid could open his mouth, the little black boy punched him in the head. Down went Pudgy with the black kid on top of him, punching away.

I was just thinking that I should go do something when I was thrown up against the wall by the other five guys. The girl was behind them, grinning. As I raised my fists, I heard *click*, and suddenly two switchblades were inches from my face. I put my hands down. The girl giggled. In the meantime the small boy had let up on Pudgy, picked up a black case, and quickly walked away. The others followed him, making me one lucky bastard. The boy could easily have swiped my face with one of those knives. It was then I realized that the small kid had just stolen Pudgy's clarinet, which was an enormous problem for Pudgy since the school had an ironclad rule about not taking instruments off the property. Pudgy ran off, presumably to face the music.

But, oh, the music at that school! I'd never heard classical music except for the few times I'd glimpsed the NBC Symphony Orchestra playing for radio broadcasts. And there I was, sitting in the school auditorium listening to guest conductor Leopold Stokowski conduct the senior orchestra in Tchaikovsky's *Overture to Romeo and Juliet*. And before long I was standing in the tenor section of the school choir at Carnegie Hall singing the "Hallelujah Chorus" from Handel's *Messiah* with the NBC orchestra conducted by none other than Toscanini himself.

I developed a lifelong love of classical music and am eternally grateful for the two years I spent at Music and Art. When I got the job in *Life with Father*, my first Broadway show, the school wouldn't let me out for matinees, so I had to leave Music and Art. My voice was not of classical caliber, so that was no great loss. What I did lose was two more years of learning how classical music is structured and how to listen to it. And the instrument I was required to learn to play in my second year at school was the viola. What I would give now to be able to play the viola. Still, I can listen to the themes and variations in Bach's solo piano works or the inner voices in symphonies in a way that I would never have been able to do without those two years.

And it certainly came in handy years later when I was a replacement in Stephen Sondheim's *A Little Night Music* on Broadway and I had to go on without any orchestra rehearsals. My training had taught my ear to recognize where the instruments would come in the orchestration. Conductor Paul Gemignani was masterful, by the way, getting me through that with only a piano run-through.

Irene, meanwhile, continued to scour the newspapers for any showbiz news, and she came across an item that said they were casting a tour of *Life with Father* and were auditioning boys to add to the company. She told me she wanted me to look into it. I was fifteen. I had never talked to Irene about "girls." I had a strong feeling that she wouldn't approve of my dating. So I didn't mention to her that on the same day I was to go over to Rockefeller Center to see about being interviewed, I also had a date to go swimming in a pool at the St. George Hotel in Brooklyn with a girl who I was dying to see in a bathing suit.

I was confident that I could handle both events and took the poor girl along with me to 30 Rockefeller Plaza. I told her to wait downstairs in the concourse, that I'd only be a few minutes. Up I went to the office of Oscar Serlin, the producer of the extraordinarily successful production of *Life with Father*, still the longest running Broadway play of all time.

The woman in the outer office said, "Are you here to see about the road company?" I had no idea what a road company was.

"Yes," I said.

"Do you have an appointment?"

"Huh, no."

She looked at me for a moment and said, "Wait here." She got up from her desk and went into Mr. Serlin's office.

Later I learned that she had told Mr. Serlin there was a boy outside who didn't have an appointment but looked about the right age to understudy the characters John and Clarence (the two eldest sons in the play). He told her he might as well have a look at me, and she came out to retrieve me. I followed her back into Mr. Serlin's office.

"Been in any Broadway plays?" Mr. Serlin asked while looking me over.

"No, sir."

"Off-Broadway?"

"No, sir."

"Plays at school?"

"Huh—no, sir."

"Any plays at all?"

"No, sir, you see I'm a song-and-dance man."

He looked at me for a moment and started to laugh.

"You remind me of me when I first came to New York. Okay . . . go down to the Empire Theatre. They're auditioning right now. Tell them I sent you."

Now what was I supposed to do? And where was the Empire Theatre? What would I tell the girl? I figured I had better call Irene, so I found a pay phone in the lobby.

"Mom, they want me to go to someplace called the Empire Theatre," I said.

"So go," Mom said.

"I don't know where it is," I said.

"Look it up in the phone book," she said.

So I sent my date home and went to the Empire. I know, at this point, I must sound like some kind of idiot. Did it never occur to me to tell my mother I didn't want to do this? The kindest thing I can say on my own behalf is that I was a young man who, from a very early age, was taught to take directions from a mother I must have loved or feared very much. Probably both. This was the pattern of my life throughout my childhood, in the army, and even in college: following someone else's instructions or suggestions without instigating anything myself. I noticed that I was able to break the pattern when I finally learned to say no, and that became a lifelong pattern in and of itself.

The stage door of the Empire was on West Forty-First Street. You entered a small vestibule; in front of you was another door; to the right of it on the wall hung a box containing the keys to the dressing rooms upstairs. Next to it was a call box hooked up to the dressing rooms; it was used to call the actors to the stage at curtain time. The small hall on the right contained two of the larger dressing rooms reserved for the stars, and a staircase led to the dressing rooms above. No one was in the vestibule, but I heard voices so I opened the door in front of me and entered into the darkness of backstage.

Now, when I told Mr. Serlin that I had never been in a play, I had failed to mention that I had never even *seen* a play. So you might say I entered that darkness timidly. I must admit that it pains me to write this; looking back on it I consider myself such a fool.

As my eyes became accustomed to the dark I could see a light ahead—the stage, as it turned out. Someone came to me and handed me a little blue book.

"You're here to read for the part of John, right?" he said.

Having no idea, I mumbled something that he must have taken as a response.

"You'll be up next."

Inside the blue book, which I still have, thanks to Irene, was a scene between John and Mary, two of the young people in the play. There would be a heading that said "Mary," then some words, then a heading that said "John," and then some more words. Before I could get through any of these few pages the gentleman came over and said, "Okay, come with me."

He led me onto the stage. The onstage furniture was covered in white sheets; it looked like a graveyard. But there was one piece uncovered, a small settee on which sat a young woman. She patted the spot next to her and I sat down. She started the scene, and whenever she stopped talking I said my lines. I held the blue book close to my nose because the lighting was so dim. I don't see how anyone there could have seen my face.

We weren't very far into the scene when I heard some laughter from out in the darkness. We stopped and a man came down the center aisle, chuckling.

"Those were Clarence's lines you just read," the man said. It seems another character had entered into the room and I had read his lines as well as my own. "Okay, I think this will work. We'll need your folks to sign a release so you can be with us on the tour."

"The tour?" I said.

"That's right; our road company will open in Boston two weeks from today. Why don't you and your folks come to see the show tomorrow night? We'll have some tickets waiting for you."

Now this may seem like a pretty casual way of hiring someone, particularly a fifteen-year-old who had walked in off the street, alone. But remember, this was 1942. Television was in its infancy. Radio was still the chief recreation in the home. More than one hundred shows opened in New York on Broadway that year, and there were many more legitimate theaters in cities across the country. Touring companies were very popular. *Life with Father* often had two or three road tours out simultaneously.

Irene and I went to the theater the next evening. My dad stayed home with the girls. We had box seats, right of the stage and very close. There I sat, about to see my first play ever and already hired to be in it. Or so I thought; I was actually to be an assistant stage manager and understudy to the two eldest sons of the Day family, John and Clarence.

The house was full, the lights went down, and in utter darkness the curtain rose. What can I say? I blinked, the bright stage lights made everything look like a twinkling jewel box, and there was the living room of the Day family. Downstage right, sitting in a wing-back chair, was Father Day, hidden behind his daily newspaper. Suddenly, still behind the newspaper, he roared "Oh God!" stamping one of his feet, and the audience roared with laughter. Magic.

Life with Father had an unprecedented seven-year run—still a record. Hardly ever produced anymore, the play was a snapshot of a family in the 1890s headed by a father whose impossible standards create humorous situations with all of the other characters in the show. It was the first sitcom, if you will. And America loved it.

The show was going on to Boston, to another charming theater, the Colonial, and I was to go with them.

That was the first shock: learning that I was going on the road alone. The next came when I was told to go to Anthony & Joseph's beauty salon on Madison Avenue to have my dark brown hair dyed a bright red. Only Father and Mother Day were afforded wigs, so all the boys had to have their hair dyed red. Of course I went along with it. At this point, it had all happened so fast that I must have been close to comatose.

I stayed in a small boardinghouse on Beacon Hill. It was wartime and Boston was filled with sailors. From Beacon Hill I had to walk through the Common to get to the theater, and there were sailors on shore leave hanging around the park benches. The first time they saw me and my flaming red hair, they whistled and yelled, "Hi, sweetheart." After that I bought a woolen stocking cap and never appeared in public without it.

After Boston our next stop on the tour was New Haven, where I received a call from Irene saying that my sisters and I had gotten an offer to do a radio show for more money than I was making in the play (my salary was $57.50 a week). Irene told me to hand in my two weeks' notice. And of course I promptly did.

Our next stop was Providence, Rhode Island, where I was back-stage calling, "Half hour, please," when I ran into our producer, Oscar Serlin.

"Hey, you've given in your notice," he said in a rather incredulous voice.

"My sisters and I have been offered our own radio program, *The Daniels Family Radio Show*, which means we'll all be working together." I didn't mention the additional money.

He looked at me, shook his head.

"Come see me when you get back to New York." And that's exactly what I did.

There was a natural progression for the two eldest boys in the play. The one playing Clarence, the eldest son, would play the part until he turned eighteen, and then he would be drafted into the armed forces. Then the young man playing John would move up to playing Clarence. The assistant stage manager/understudy would get his chance to play John. That's what happened to me.

I began to think of myself as an actor, not just a song-and-dance man. And not just an actor but a man on his own, free from his family a lot of the time, going to school in the city, hanging around alone after school until it was time to go to the theater. I spent a lot of time in coffee shops with names like Chock full o'Nuts, sipping coffee and reading the *New York Times*. From the time I was fifteen until I was drafted into the army at eighteen, I learned a lot of things and lost some things, too. I learned the discipline it takes to be in a play, the concentration and focus it requires to be on stage with an ear open to your audience's reaction, the proper behavior and deportment backstage, the proper way to gauge a laugh and when to cut into it. I also lost some things; as I mentioned, I never completed my education at the High School of Music and Art, and I lost my virginity to a girl in the play.

I was fifteen; "Eve" (I'll call her) was twenty. Eve played the ingénue and the romantic interest of the eldest son, Clarence. And although she was much older than I was, she was also my romantic interest. As for the sex, I'd never seen a naked woman. Without saying more, I'll just note that this woman taught me to put the proper things in the proper places.

She lived at the Rehearsal Club for Women, which allowed no men above the first-floor sitting room. So most of our activities took place in her dressing room at the theater before anyone arrived for the show. At one point we got careless, and at the start of a performance with the curtain already up I found myself on top of the dear girl on the floor of her dressing room (in flagrante, as Maupassant would say) when I heard a voice shout up from the stairwell, "Daniels, you're on!" I was caught with the proverbial pants down. And these pants, being part of an authentic turn-of-the-century costume, had no zipper, just a series of hard-to-cope-with buttons on the fly that seemed to take forever to get buttoned up as I stumbled down the stairs to the stage. This delayed my entrance even further.

Dear, kind, gentle Dorothy Stickney, playing my mother, was upstage looking off into the wings, waiting patiently for me. And only when I arrived, wide-eyed, did she say, "Oh, there you are!"

Eve helped me lose my Catholic faith as well, something I've never regretted. My mother had been pestering me to go to confession at church during Lent. Walking down Fifth Avenue with my ingénue, I noticed a Catholic church.

"Listen, let's stop in here for a minute," I said.

I showed her to a back pew and went forward and entered the confessional.

"Forgive me, Father, for I have sinned." I always made things up, since I didn't feel particularly guilty about anything, or I'd just mention a litany of minor offenses: lies, masturbation, sex.

The priest sat in the dark on the other side of the screen. I can only imagine that he recognized bull when he heard it.

"Say ten 'Hail Marys' and ten 'Our Fathers.'"

And that was it. I went out into a pew, crossed myself, and said the prayers of penance.

Then I retrieved my girlfriend and out we went.

"What did you confess?" she asked.

"What do you mean?"

"What did you confess?" she said again.

"Oh, you know, the usual things . . . I lied here or there, curse words, stuff like that."

"You confessed me, didn't you?" Of course I had.

Then it struck me, right there on Fifth Avenue, the hypocrisy of confessing to something that was so lovely and innocent. It was absurd.

And for me that was the end of Catholicism, with its idea of original sin. I didn't enter a Catholic church again, not until Irene's funeral many years later.

Howard Lindsay was coauthor with Russel Crouse of *Life with Father*, and he was the play's original Father Day—a role he played for hundreds and hundreds of performances. Although I'm sure he was never aware of it, he became my unofficial mentor and model for how to behave onstage and off. I came upon him once at four in the afternoon, hours before curtain, sitting in his chair onstage with only a naked bulb on a stand in center stage. He was practicing his opening speech. He and his wife, Dorothy Stickney, were coming back into the play after having taken a long hiatus. And I was fortunate enough to be entering the cast in the role of John, the second oldest son, and therefore had the great opportunity of rehearsing with them as they refreshed their memory by walking through their starring roles.

At one point in our rehearsing Mr. Lindsay stopped in a scene with me and said, "Bill, I'm not saying this because I wrote the play with Russel, but we have more laughs in this play than we need, more than enough to keep the audience happy, but we must not wear them out. Rather, send them home feeling that they haven't laughed enough; so, when this line I say to you comes, it will get a big laugh—the laugh will build and build, then level off and start to come down. That's where I want you to say your line, not when the laugh has worn itself out. Watch my eyes and they will tell you when to speak." And it never failed; night after night, laugh after laugh, his eyes released me to speak.

Through those instructions from Howard Lindsay I learned to listen to my fellow actor, to look him in the eyes, to listen to the audience's response, and to time a laugh.

Playing eight performances a week in those days, and for many years after, presented no problem for me. Today I shudder at the thought. In the 1950s and 1960s David Merrick, the prolific Broadway producer, was asking actors to sign two-year contracts. I played John Adams in the Broadway production of *1776* for two years and three months. And in that role you never left the stage—at first there wasn't even an intermission, but after a couple of months they added an intermission to sell concessions.

Today actors in Broadway shows sign three- and four-month contracts, six months at the most. But even so, playing the role of John Adams, even for that long, was a great time for me. There is no greater satisfaction for an actor than performing before a live audience, to cope with an audience from the beginning of a performance to the end. First they may be coughing, rustling in their seats, flipping pages in their programs, and wondering if the play is going to be worth the price of the tickets. And then you slowly but surely command their attention with your stage presence, your focus, and your conviction. Finally it is so quiet you know you have their full attention. You can let your acting impulses take over and carry you wherever they will, for as far as the audience is concerned you can do no wrong.

I got a terrific sense of instant satisfaction and of power, if you will, playing John Adams. Having seen Mr. Lindsay do it, night after night, I'm sure he also felt that while playing in *Life with Father*. Of course with power comes responsibility. I learned this from watching him. You give each performance your best; you don't dog it, you don't walk through a performance. You give the audience the best you've got—every time. Sure, some nights, many nights, you're not happy with your performance and you promise yourself to try to do better, but these are personal goals that actors set for themselves and that most of us never entirely reach.

I played John and then Clarence in *Life with Father* for more than two years. Of course there was always in my mind the awareness that when I turned eighteen I would be drafted into the army. With that in mind, I sought out Mr. Lindsay's advice.

I knocked on his dressing room door and heard his imperious Father Day voice cry out, "Come in!"

I timidly approached.

"I wanted to ask you for some advice."

"Go ahead."

"I'll probably be drafted into the army soon, and I was wondering—do you think it might be a good idea, after my army service, to enroll in the American Academy of Dramatic Arts?"

He looked at me in his mirror while applying a makeup base to his face.

"Close the door," he said.

I closed the door and went to stand next to him, so we were both looking at him in his makeup mirror.

"Bill, I'm on the board of the academy. Don't go there." He turned toward me. "Find a college or university that has a good theater department where you can study not just acting but all the factors that go into a theater production—sets, lighting, costumes, and directing. And at the same time you'll get a college education." And two years later that's exactly what I did.

Mr. Lindsay, I think, was the greatest male influence in my life. It's because of him that I have spent my life emulating his stage presence, playing upper-class, patrician roles. No, I never played a bricklayer, so *Life with Father* turned out to be life with a kind of "father" indeed.

4

Offstage in the Theater of War

From the age of four I'd never had an extended break from performing. It would take a war to give me what amounted to a two-year vacation from show business—a world war, to be exact. As the time approached for me to report to the induction center on Lexington Avenue and Forty-Third Street for a physical examination, I made arrangements to leave *Life with Father* a week before my appointment, so I would have time to get my hair dyed back to its original color from that flaming red I'd been hiding under a cap for two years. But before I could play my last performance, my replacement, Harvey Collins, who would be moving up from John to Clarence, sent word that he had sustained a third-degree sunburn while relaxing out on Long Island. That meant of course that I had to continue performing and appear for my physical at the induction center as a flaming redhead!

All the inductees were lined up in front of a long bench and told to strip. A captain came walking down the line, glancing at each of us, and when he came to me he stopped, looked at my head and then down at my crotch. He pulled me out of the line.

"Come with me," he said. I thought, *Oh Harvey, when I get a hold of you, I'll wring your neck!* The captain took me to his office, told me to sit down, sat behind his desk, put his feet up, and stared at me. I wondered how to look innocent, confident, a victim of circumstances, and blasé when nude. Do you cross your legs, cover your crotch with your hands, or maybe cross your arms and play with your earlobe? He stared at me for quite some time and then he said, "Let me guess . . . *Life with Father*?"

A theatergoer. Thank God!

"Yes, sir. Thank you, sir." I said.

"And you like girls, right?" he said.

"Oh, yes, sir! Very much so, sir," I replied.

"Wait a minute. I've got to show the guys this." He left the office, only to come back with two other officers, who looked at me and chuckled. "And he likes girls!" the captain said.

All I could do was sit there with a goofy grin on my face.

Several weeks later I found myself at Fort Dix in New Jersey, standing on one long line after another to be issued a uniform, army boots, and other items, along with a duffel bag to carry them in. Dinner was cafeteria style, with largely forgettable food, and then it was on to a bunk bed in a huge Quonset hut that must have held a hundred beds. I went through it all in a robotic trance. I was told to go here, go there, stand here, and stand there—I was used to all of that coming from Irene and from Howard Lindsay. Only now I had total anonymity. That's a strange feeling for a performer who is used to a certain celebrity.

I lay awake in a bunk, staring into the dark. I finally fell asleep, and in the morning I was jarred awake by a voice over the PA system.

"Drop your cocks and grab your socks," it screamed.

Oh Lord, what am I into here? I thought.

Several days later I was on a troop train with compartments holding double bunk beds, four beds to a cabin, heading west. I had no idea where we were going. None of us did. It was hot on the train, no air-conditioning, so we traveled all night with the window open. I remember the next morning seeing the shape of my head outlined on the pillow in black soot.

As I stood on line waiting to get into the train's bathroom to wash my blackened face, I thought, *Good Lord, where are we going?* It turned out that our destination was Little Rock, Arkansas, where buses took us out to Camp Joseph T. Robinson for sixteen weeks of infantry basic training.

The camp was a series of dirt roads, Quonset huts on stilts, public latrines, mess halls, and officer headquarters. It was July, and it was hot. My Quonset hut held twelve to fourteen double bunks, and I was fortunate enough to have a thirty-four-year-old engineer from Wilmington, Delaware, as my bunkmate. He had been caught just under the upper draft age limit. He was a wise and practical man who accepted his fate with resigned equanimity, though he was in no physical condition to withstand the training we were about to embark on—in the middle of July. Most of the other inductees in our barracks were pleasant southern boys.

For some reason the lieutenant in charge of our squad made me an acting sergeant and gave me a black armband that said so. All this meant was that I was to march my squad in formation, in, out, and around camp, keeping them in a neat line with me marching on the outside of them, keeping cadence with *hup, two, three, four . . . hup, two, three, four. To the right flank, harch* (not march). *To the left flank, harch.* And then, *halt* and *at ease.* I rather enjoyed this.

I looked after my men, tied neckties for those who had never owned a necktie, and made sure they'd all pass inspection. Still, forced marching up into the hills of Arkansas in the heat of summer was no easy matter. There was a truck that followed along to pick up those who couldn't make it. I'm afraid my engineer buddy was among them.

I can't say I was a good soldier. I was a terrible marksman with an M1 rifle, whose kick gave me a swollen lip, but I did finally make the grade. I didn't mind the routine, policing the area for stray cigarette butts and "field stripping" them—separating the tobacco from the paper and throwing them out separately—KP duty, even thrusting my bayonet into a dummy, though I knew I'd never be able to do that to a human being.

Fortunately I wouldn't have to; Germany had capitulated, and while we were in training the bombs were dropped on Hiroshima and Nagasaki.

Looking back, I realize I was quite happy just being one of the guys, away from performing, away from being the arbiter and peacemaker in my family. Free of all that! I was my own man! Granted, I sent my laundry home every couple of weeks, which my mother returned freshly laundered, but other than that—*completely* independent.

At the end of sixteen weeks I had a PFC stripe on my arm, an M1 rifle that I knew how to clean, oil, and reassemble, and a bunk bed made up so taut that the captain could bounce a dime on it.

The next stop was an overcrowded troopship leaving from Newport News and headed to Italy. We were to be a part of the U.S. forces of occupation. The hold with the sleeping quarters on the ship had eight bunk beds stacked on top of each other. I was given a lower bunk, but a guy at the top got seasick, so I found a spot on the crowded deck and that's where I stayed for the rest of the voyage.

We landed at Naples and were immediately put on a train headed for Gorizia, an Italian town at the foot of the Alps. We were to stand guard in case there was trouble over who was to control the open city of Trieste. Halfway up the coast, at the town of Livorno, the train stopped and a sergeant came walking down the aisle calling out my name.

"Yo," I said. He told me to follow him. We got off the train and into his jeep and drove off, leaving all my buddies behind. The sergeant said nothing. I said nothing.

I'd become accustomed to not knowing where I was going (that my platoon was headed to Gorizia was something I had learned after the fact). We wound up in front of a two-story building with a high wall around it. This building had been a former Gestapo headquarters, but now it was a radio station for the Armed Forces Radio Service. And this is where I remained for the rest of my stay in Italy. It turned out that my army paperwork had my MOS (military occupational specialty) as "entertainer," so even though I thought I had gotten away from it all, the army had decided that I needed to be back in the radio business.

When I arrived at the radio station, it was manned by combat veterans from General Mark Clark's Thirty-Fourth Division who were waiting orders to be shipped back home. These were the heroes who had liberated North Africa and Rome.

The combat veterans left one by one and were replaced by new recruits, and in a matter of months I was a staff sergeant in charge of running the station. Our captain was holed up in the officers' apartment building with his Italian mistress and rarely appeared at the station. When he did, he didn't stay long. I devised the programming schedule, assigned announcers to run the shows, made certain our prerecorded V-discs were picked up at the army post office, and in short enjoyed every minute of it.

Our backyard at the station had a walk-in bar stocked with lots of booze—cheap stuff shipped over from the States. There were colored lanterns hanging from the trees, a hammock, and tables and chairs, and music from upstairs in the studio played on outdoor speakers. A lot of officers, some with dates, hung out here on the weekends. I used the setting in an attempt to attract a rather cultured-looking Italian girl, only to find out that she was pining for a German officer who was in the POW camp just outside of town.

All this booze, as well as ice cream and other items, was sent over from the supply depot, and in return we cut discs for them, recording their voices with messages to their families or girlfriends. They could also call up at any time to request a song to be played over the air to impress whomever they were with. *Quid pro quo.*

I traveled quite a bit during the year and a half that I was in Livorno. I spent a week of R&R (recreation and rehabilitation—but from what?) in Switzerland and was put up and fed in only the top-notch hotels. There were weekend trips to Florence and Siena. I finagled a remote broadcast from Rome commemorating Pope Pius XII coming out of hiding from his lake retreat somewhere up north. I had heard a rumor that this pope was an anti-Semite and Nazi sympathizer. Whether or not it was true, it drove the final nail into the coffin of Catholicism for me; I was finished with it.

Despite that, I wanted to have a beautiful pair of bone-carved rosary beads blessed by the pope for my grandmother, Big Gram. I'd bought the rosary beads in Florence with her in mind. I knew she would be thrilled. Getting those beads blessed required pushing up front in a huge crowd and kneeling at the altar rail with others who visited for a papal blessing. As I knelt there, rosary hanging from my hand, I noticed that as the pope walked down the line blessing each supplicant, he held out his hand with a huge ring on it to be kissed.

I have a thing about germs, inherited from my father, who never used a public toilet unless he only had to urinate. What to do? When the pope pushed his hand in front of my face, I missed the ring altogether and just brushed his hand lightly against my cheek. He touched the rosary, made the sign of the cross, and mumbled something. So despite my loss of faith and my germophobia, I managed to obtain a rosary with a papal blessing. My grandmother would be ecstatic when she received it.

When my year and a half in Italy was over, I was marched onto a troopship much like the one I'd come over on and sailed home. On the ship I met my old platoon buddies, who had spent the year and a half guarding Trieste, often in trenches. I took a lot of teasing about my staff sergeant stripes.

I was never homesick while in Livorno. I never once wrote home nor did I speak on the phone with my mother, who had become the chief telephone operator at Fort Tilden in Far Rockaway, New York.

I never even wrote to Eve, the girl I'd been seeing during *Life with Father*. I had an out-of-sight-out-of-mind mentality that stuck with me even later, when I was a married man and went on the road as an actor.

As I mentioned, I did send my laundry home in a plastic box twice a month. And the box was promptly returned with clean clothes and often with some goodies—a salami or a carton of cigarettes, which I promptly sold on the black market.

Before I left for the army, Eve had had plans for me: we were to be married, we would establish residence in Illinois, and I was to go to the University of Illinois to study medicine. No doubt her enthusiasm waned when she didn't hear from me for two years. When I got home and found that she'd moved on and was in the middle of a relationship, I was both naïvely surprised and deeply relieved.

As I headed home, I didn't know what Irene's plans for me were and I didn't care. I would have no more of that. I was a free man about to call my own shots.

5

Go West, Young Man, to Northwestern

My dad met me at the troopship and suggested we go to Chicago to see my sisters. My younger sister Carol had a rather large role in a touring company of the play *Apple of His Eye*, starring Walter Huston. My sister Jackie was understudying the ingénue lead, and my mother was in the lobby selling programs. I was still in uniform when I walked into the lobby and saw her. I stopped in my tracks.

"Now, Billy, don't be mad. I'm only doing this to hear what the audiences at intermissions have to say about Carol's performance," Irene said.

Of course, Mr. Huston, who loved my sisters, loved my mother even more for doing this. It really tickled him.

I saw Carol perform and she was good. She was also nine years old and scared to death at each performance. She once wrote in lipstick on the dressing room towel, "I'm so *skerd* [sic]." And on the dressing room mirror after the show she wrote, "I was so bad." Irene promised Carol and Jackie a puppy in situations like this if they'd just keep going—but the dog never materialized.

A word about Walter Huston. He took the play on the road not only so that his friend, Jed Harris, who produced it, could recoup his investment but also because Huston was a man of the theater (in addition to film) who loved performing in front of a live audience. At the end of the play he always sang "September Song" to the accompaniment of the ingénue's guitar—to cover, he would tell the audience, the tax the audience paid on their tickets. I don't know if it was because I was still in uniform or that he learned that I'd been in *Life with Father* or both, but he took me under his wing for that brief time that we were together.

"*Life with Father*," he said. "I was offered the role of Father and I turned it down. One of the big mistakes of my career! And I was asked to invest in it and turned that down. How long did it run?"

"Seven years on Broadway," I replied.

Huston went on, "I accepted the title role in that great Shakespeare play *Macbeth* in a Broadway production. I immersed myself in the part. I took a hotel room across from the theater. I went from the hotel to the theater and back for weeks. I saw no one, just reread the play at night in my hotel room, memorized the lines. We opened on Broadway, and after the performance I saw no one, went to no opening night parties, simply rushed back to the hotel to await the reviews. They were brought to me as soon as they came out, and I sat in bed and read one bad review after another. All of them awful. And when I finished reading them I started to laugh and couldn't stop. 'Of course,' I said to myself. 'You were terrible!'"

While *Apple of His Eye* was in Detroit Mr. Huston received word from his son John that they were ready to begin shooting a film in which Walter had promised to appear. "My crazy son," he called John (because of his leftist politics). But, because of the film, Walter Huston had to close the play prematurely.

Then, with the help of Jed Harris and his manager, Mr. Huston phoned every connection they could think of to get every actor in the show a job. My sister Carol met with a top Hollywood casting director. After Mr. Huston called the Langners of the Theatre Guild, for whom he had appeared in *Knickerbocker Holiday*, my sister Jackie wound up playing Ado Annie in the London company of *Oklahoma!* That was the sort of man Walter Huston was. You may have guessed that the film he went to do for his son was the classic *The Treasure of the Sierra Madre*.

Back at the Chicago hotel where the family was staying Irene said, "I think one of those colleges you mentioned is around here somewhere."

While I was in Italy I had followed up on Howard Lindsay's advice to find a college and had written to the Office of Education in Washington. They recommended four universities with outstanding theater departments: Yale, Catholic University, UCLA, and Northwestern.

We asked the hotel concierge.

"Northwestern? Sure it's in Evanston. Just take the 'L' up there."

The "L" was a train that ran on elevated tracks and I took it. After wandering around the most beautiful campus I'd ever seen, not that I'd ever seen a college campus before, I found the admissions office. I told a person behind a desk I was interested in studying acting and theater. When I mentioned that I had acted on Broadway in *Life with Father*, the person became interested, and I suppose my army uniform worked in my favor, too. The man at the desk sent me to another building to take an entrance exam.

I hesitated. "An exam?" I said.

"Go on, they're starting the exam in a few minutes."

What can I say—I went. I found the room where a number of other would-be students sat and was handed an exam. It looked like a book—and not a short one. I sat at a desk and started to slowly read and write. Most of the questions were just true or false, but I found some very puzzling. Could be true, could be false. I pondered. Time went by and then I heard a voice.

"Are you finished?"

I looked up and saw that the room was empty—just me and the guy who was running the exam. I had only made it through a little more than half the pages.

"Uh, well, yeah—I guess so." I handed him the whole thing. I left, got back on the L, sat down, and said to myself, "Well, that's that. I'll never get into that place."

I did get in, but only because of several odd occurrences. The university sent application papers to the two high schools I had attended. The High School of Music and Art returned my scholastic records for the two years that I spent there. The university also sent application papers to Lodge Private Tutoring, the "school" I went to for my last two years of high school, while I was in *Life with Father*. Lodge was merely a large living room in an apartment on West Fifty-Sixth Street where a handful of youngsters, all working in the theater, were tutored by a couple of teachers. I remember trying to figure out trigonometry with Mr. Brentano, one of the teachers, but neither he nor I could make heads or tails of it, so we gave up.

I had a phone call from Mr. Lodge, of Lodge Private Tutoring, who, in a surprised tone of voice, said, "You're applying to college? I just received a request from Northwestern for your school grades."

From his tone it appeared that he didn't get such requests very often.

"Yes, sir, they want my high school records," I replied.

"I see," he said. "Well, you see, unfortunately last year we had a fire here at the school and all of the records were destroyed. I'm sorry."

"Oh my God, Mr. Lodge, I need those records in order to be accepted." There was a pause.

"You don't happen to remember any of your grades, do you?" he asked.

A lightbulb went on over my head just like in the comic books.

"Well, yeah—I think I might remember some," I answered.

"How about English?" he asked.

"I was pretty good at English. I got a ninety I think."

"How about American history?"

At this point I should have realized Mr. Lodge was in on the scam; they didn't teach American history at Lodge Private Tutoring. I, who went on to play John Adams in front of thousands of people, had never taken American history.

"I think I got an eighty-five," I said.

And so he went down the list of subjects. I wasn't greedy. I gave myself average scores and Mr. Lodge sent them in. To this day I still don't know if there had actually been a fire at that "school."

Another strange thing happened concerning my matriculation. I needed three years of a language. I'd twice flunked Spanish at Music and Art. So that summer I entered the Berlitz School for Languages. My teacher was a middle-aged, bald-headed man in glasses who on the first day stood in front of the class of some thirty students of various ages and said, "You're all here because you're stupid. I've been teaching third-year Spanish for twenty years, and no matter how stupid you are, if you do exactly as I say, you *will* pass the New York State Regents Exam for third-year Spanish."

He explained that we would have to memorize a series of nouns and verbs along with some colloquial expressions that invariably appear on the exam. But the main portion, the big point-getter, would be writing an essay. He had made a twenty-year study of the essay topics—things like "How I met my best friend" or "How I spent last summer." I chose "How I met my best friend."

Here's the way it worked: the teacher helped you write your first version. You took it home, memorized it, returned to class the next day, and wrote out the version you'd memorized. He corrected that second version. You went home and repeated the process with a third version, which he inspected for corrections. You were now ready: you had your essay memorized and ready to go. So, as in my case, the topic that appeared on the exam was "How I spent last summer." I wrote, "Last summer I went to camp and met my best friend . . ." I followed it of course with my memorized essay about my best friend and ended with "and that's how I spent last summer." I lost two points on the first sentence and two points on the last, and I came out with thirty-six points. *The man was a genius.* I passed my State Regents Exam in third-year Spanish. If you were thinking there was something not quite kosher in all of this, you'd be right. But in 1947 it got me into Northwestern University, one of the best schools in the country.

The campus was magnificent, particularly in the eyes of a kid from Brooklyn: Gothic-style buildings, a row of fraternity buildings on the street opposite sorority houses, and private homes that always had rooms for students to rent. And of course it all fronted on beautiful Lake Michigan.

Harry Westerfield, a friend who knew my family and my sisters and me as performers, kindly arranged that I be admitted to a fraternity, Sigma Nu, without going through the rigmarole of pledge week. If I had gone through that week, I would have known that fraternities were not for me. I lived in the fraternity house for a couple of weeks before they got around to a silly initiation; they took you into the conference room and made you bend over while they paddled your behind. That did it. I left the room and yelled down the stairwell, "You can take your fraternity and shove it up your ass!"

The next day I found a room off campus and left Sigma Nu. After two years in the army I was too old for such nonsense. Besides, I had no need for that kind of fraternity. I didn't need to join a club, either to meet new buddies or to prove how much liquor I could hold.

I had a new fraternity. It was located in Annie Mae Swift Hall, the university building that housed the theater program. It was one of the oldest buildings on campus and small compared to all the other buildings. It was a two-story red stone structure that housed an auditorium with a small stage. A rather large room on the left as you entered served as a gathering place in which students could hang out between classes or just spend time with other aspiring actors. The second story consisted of classrooms and faculty offices. The auditorium with its stage housed our theater productions, as well as acting classes and something called B-40, a technical course in lighting, stage sets, and costuming. Sets were built in another building close by.

Aside from the classrooms where our required liberal arts courses met, these two buildings were where theater students spent all their time—day and night—studying acting, building sets, and appearing in productions.

I was happy to jump into all this. I have to confess I was a bit cocky. After all, I'd acted on Broadway while all the others were coming from high school productions. I attended an audition with fifteen to twenty other students, all hoping to be cast in an antiwar play by Irwin Shaw called *Bury the Dead*, in which characters rose up out of graves and told of dying in war or losing loved ones. Not a laugh in it.

We sat at desks in a classroom with the director at the head of the class calling on one student after another to read different parts. I sat up front listening to one awful reading after another. I was just thinking that I wasn't sure I wanted to be in this turkey when the director called out, "Bonnie, read the next section."

I heard the voice of a *real* actress. I turned around to look, and there in the back reading was this tall blond with a lovely voice. She was making a highly dramatic scene believable. This was a girl who was obviously talented. After the audition was over I waited at the classroom door for her to pass by.

"How about a cup of coffee?" I said.

"You're too short," she said without hesitation. *But we were exactly the same height.*

"Come on, have a cup of coffee."

"Okay."

Eventually she told me that where she came from, some place called Moline, Illinois, girls were expected to date only boys who were taller than they were. Obviously, some primitive, midwestern, unwritten law. She said she had been following *me* around campus because she had heard I had acted on Broadway. The air force leather jacket I wore didn't hurt either.

I took her to a student hangout called Cooley's Cupboard, and we joined some other students who had been at the audition. No one knew each other, and at one point during a lull in the conversation Bonnie (her last name was Bartlett) told a joke about a newly married couple in the upper berth of a train on their wedding night. Her story was greeted by utter silence. Not only was it not funny, but when I looked at her I realized she didn't know it was a dirty joke. Eighteen years old, coming out of Moline—what could you expect?

What I didn't expect was that our "coffee date" would turn into almost a seventy-year relationship—with *me* telling the jokes. We have a kind of George Burns and Gracie Allen routine. When Bonnie tries to be funny and fails, the situation can always be saved by a simple "Say goodnight, Gracie."

We'd been going together for a little while but nothing had been physical. I'd bring her flowers and serenade her with a Sinatra song or two. But it was enough to make Bonnie break up with the boyfriend she had left in Moline. On opening night of *Bury the Dead* Bonnie arrived at the theater in tears after making the "Dear John" phone call, and she was so distraught I had to do her makeup for her. The intimacy of this moment was something Bonnie wasn't used to in her life, and she remembers it as a pivotal moment in our relationship. She also remembers giving the performance of her life that night.

Although Bonnie was, and still is, a great dramatic actress, she had a problem when it came to singing. When she was in rehearsals for *Dark of the Moon*, she had to sing a song called "Barbara Allen." Singing was a challenge for Bonnie. None of the parts she had played in high school—from the title role in *I Remember Mama* to Lady Macbeth—required her to sing. In fact Bonnie had a mental block when it came to singing, so, being the old song-and-dance man, I stepped in to help her.

There were few places on campus where you could get any privacy, but Bonnie lived in Willard Hall, which had a finished basement that was used for student activities. It was usually empty, so we figured it was a good place to work on Bonnie's singing without being disturbed.

We were down there going over her song, and I could tell she had a good voice but was afraid to use it. First I tried to get her to relax, then to stand up and breathe from her diaphragm and just sing. Then I put my hands around her waist, to check her breathing. We looked at each other and I kissed her. Her knees actually buckled and I had to hold her up—but I kissed her again. The song took care of itself.

Later Bonnie was called into Miss Yearly's office (she was the dean of women) and reprimanded for necking in the basement with a New York actor. To this day we don't know who had spied on us. Miss Yearly suggested that playing Barbara Allen, a loose woman, was having a bad influence on Bonnie's behavior. She was even thinking of calling Bonnie's parents. Ah, those were the days.

In our freshman year, while I was doing a little lightweight play by actress Ruth Gordon called *Years Ago*, Bonnie won the freshman Best Actress of the Year award for her work in *Dark of the Moon*. I went to see her in the play. The famous church scene where Barbara Allen, amid a chanting crowd, is raped in order to rid her of the evil taint of consorting with her lover the "witch boy" was so compelling and shocking that I couldn't watch it and had to leave the theater.

It was at that moment that I realized I was in love with her. Our friends called us "Bill and Coo," the old-fashioned expression for hugging and kissing. We became inseparable unless we fought, which was often. Then we'd walk off in different directions and spend the rest of the day looking for each other. In retrospect I think we needed a hotel room to be alone together, but that never occurred to me and if it had, I hadn't the wherewithal to book one.

Bonnie says I was the poorest person she'd ever met. It's true I never had any cash (she even paid for us to go to the movies). But I had the GI Bill. It provided me with full tuition and books, something I never could have afforded on my own. My mother and father made it only through the eighth grade, and my sisters never graduated from high school. I worked behind the counter at the school cafeteria, and when Bonnie came in for a hamburger and a chocolate malt, I gave her a malt you could eat with a spoon. I paid for my room off campus with what I'd saved from my army pay, most of which I'd sent home to my mother. I didn't feel destitute—what more did I need? My life revolved around Annie Mae Swift Hall and the best actress in the theater department.

Bonnie came from a middle-class family, but her brother Bob was well off—he had put himself thorough college playing bridge, and he was helping turn the family insurance business into one of the biggest in Illinois. Bob would take us to nightclubs on Howard Street just outside of Chicago where I could hear the great jazz musicians of the day, including Nat King Cole, Duke Ellington, and Billie Holiday.

Bob knew them all and helped them find housing in Davenport and Moline because, as African Americans, they weren't allowed in "white" hotels. What a thrill when he invited Billie Holiday over to our table—my biggest thrill since meeting Bojangles when I was a kid. I vividly remember her onstage—beautiful, gardenia in her hair, covered with sweat while singing *Strange Fruit* and *Lover Man* as though she were singing them for me.

Bonnie and I did many plays at Northwestern—Chekhov, Ibsen, Shakespeare, and a season of summer stock in Eagles Mere, Pennsylvania, run by the school's famous acting teacher, Alvina Krause. In our senior year we played opposite each other in *Macbeth*. I'm so happy it was never recorded. God knows what that was like; actually Bonnie, being the dramatic actress she was, was good. I looked like a short-legged pumpkin in the blooming pantaloons of the costume they put me in. At a matinee in the final dueling scene between Macbeth and Macduff, my dagger hooked on his sword and flew out into the audience. We froze. Silence. I couldn't hear the dagger drop. I had a vision of the lights coming up at the end of the play with a little old lady sitting there, head drooped, a dagger in her chest. I never saw the knife again, so maybe it actually wound up in a little old lady's purse.

It was considered an honor to be chosen by Miss Krause to spend the summer in Eagles Mere doing eight or nine weeks of plays. After our sophomore year Bonnie and I were both invited. You were given room and board but nothing else. I was there because Bonnie was there—we were still tied at the hip and sexually frustrated with no relief in sight—communal living in summer stock! We each had a roommate of the same sex. I'd had enough of communal living in the army, so I made a pain in the ass of myself declaring I was the only person there who was a member in good standing of Actors' Equity and working there for no pay was making me a "scab" laborer, because you had to build the sets as well as act in the plays.

But though I complained, I did learn something about acting in that little playhouse.

It was in *A Midsummer Night's Dream*, playing one of Bottom's group of tradesmen, Starveling the tailor, and I had one line: "Here, Peter Quince." I entered in a costume of rags, wearing a dunce hat, and pulling on a string a little wooden duck that waddled (the director's idea), and in dress rehearsal my fellow actors, the crew, and the staff all fell apart laughing. On opening night I entered, pulling my little wooden duck, and was greeted with utter silence; the piece of business with the duck had nothing to do with the scene, didn't relate to it at all. The cast had been laughing at Bill Daniels, the Bill Daniels they knew, looking ridiculous in a funny costume, pulling a wooden duck. The audience didn't know Bill Daniels. It wasn't that they didn't get the joke; there was no joke to get.

Then there was Molière's *Tartuffe*, in which I played the title role. I had watched Emil Jannings's performance in the film *The Blue Angel*, which I thought had similarities to *Tartuffe*, and I fashioned my performance along those lines—big mistake! I wound up slouching around the stage, with my nose in a Bible when I wasn't leering down a woman's bodice, while wearing makeup that made me look more like Bela Lugosi in *Dracula*. I don't remember getting any laughs. As far as my performance was concerned, the audience could have been comatose. The lesson? Don't copy someone else's performance, stick with what you've got—your own capabilities, your own instrument—and if you're lucky enough not to be miscast (as I was in *Tartuffe*), you might come up with something presentable.

As you must have guessed, I was a poor student academically. In the four courses that I took in my first quarter at Northwestern I got an A, B, C, and D. The A was in a theater course. During semester break I showed the grades to my father.

"That's a nice sampling," he said. No doubt any dry wit I have came from him.

Since neither of my parents got past the eighth grade, I'm sure college (which they had never suggested) was a mystery to them. It was Bonnie who got me through it, and by taking extra classes and summer school we graduated in three and a half years. She insisted that I attend all classes even though I was inclined to skip some, especially if we were being tested on material I hadn't gotten around to reading. Bonnie taught me how to study and underline what was important so that I could go back and review to prepare for the exam. My grades improved to the point that by my senior year they were better than Bonnie's, and I was awarded a scholarship to study for a master's degree and become an acting assistant to Alvina Krause, truly a great honor. With that good fortune came a big decision: to stay in school or go to New York.

"I'm going to New York," said Bonnie.

By now I assumed we would be married. So did she, I think, although I don't remember asking her to marry me. I wasn't going to let her go to New York alone, so I passed on the scholarship. I had hesitated in making my decision because I loved being part of the great program at Northwestern. Many who graduated from the program there went on to have great careers in theater, film, and TV—Charlton Heston, Patricia Neal, and Cloris Leachman had just left when we arrived there. Charlotte Rae and Paul Lynde were seniors. Right after us came Richard Benjamin and Paula Prentiss. Later alums include the actor and playwright George Furth, Nancy Dussault, and Stephen Colbert. But many of the most talented actors I worked with at the school never became professional actors or they went into the business for only a short time. It's a tough business.

And I knew what awaited us in New York. It was a tough town Bonnie and I were entering. I'd been away for more than five years, and I no longer had any connections.

1. Irene and Charlie Daniels, my parents, in their wedding photo, 1917.
Courtesy of author.

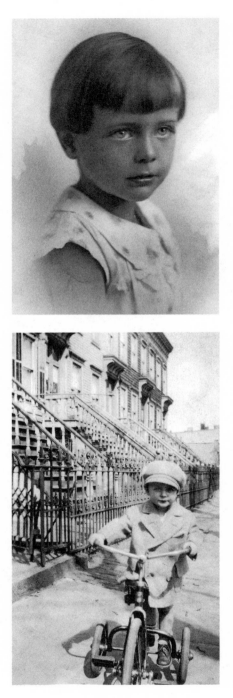

2. Billy Daniels, 1929 (age two). Courtesy of author.

3. Billy Daniels on a bike in Brooklyn, 1931 (age four). Courtesy of author.

4. Early headshot of Billy and Jackie Daniels (ages nine and seven). Courtesy of author.

5. Poster of Billy and Jackie Daniels (ages fourteen and twelve). Courtesy of author.

6. Billy, Jackie, and Carol Daniels (ages fifteen, thirteen, and five). Courtesy of author.

7. Billy and Jackie Daniels, radio show. Courtesy of author.

8. Billy in *Life with Father*, credited as "William Daniels" (age fifteen). Photograph by Vandamm Studio. © The New York Public Library.

9. Army Staff Sergeant William Daniels, DJing in Italy (age eighteen). Courtesy of author.

10. Bill and Bonnie Bartlett Daniels, wedding picture, 1951. Courtesy of author.

11. *Seagulls Over Sorrento*, Theatre Guild production, 1952. Photograph by Fred Fehl, courtesy of Gabriel Pinski.

12. William Daniels and George
Maharis in *The Zoo Story*, 1960.
Courtesy of author.

13. (*Above*) The Strasberg family outside the Actors Studio, 1960. Courtesy of author.

14. (*Opposite top*) William Daniels as Captain Nice (promo photo), 1967. Source: NBC Universal.

15. (*Opposite bottom*) William Daniels in *The Graduate* (production still), 1967. Courtesy of author.

16. William Daniels in *The
Graduate* (costume fitting),
1967. Courtesy of author.

6

If I Can Make It There

A "catch-22" situation exists for actors: you need an agent to represent you and submit your name for jobs, but agents are only interested in actors who are already working. Still, off we went to New York with no representation, and within a year we were married.

When I announced to my parents that I was going to marry Bonnie, my mother went to bed for three days.

My father came to me and said, "You're killing your mother."

That of course was not literally true, but the clash of religions—the Catholic Daniels family versus the Protestant Bartletts—wasn't exactly calculated to win any points with my mother. The religion issue was resolved by Bonnie writing the ceremony herself. We also had to agree to be married in Bonnie's hometown of Moline, Illinois—the home of John Deere plows and the place where the Mississippi runs east to west. The *Moline Dispatch* announced that ours was "a wedding in the glen," which was in actuality the Bartlett backyard. It was a nondenominational ceremony conducted by an Illinois judge subsequently disbarred for fraud. I refuse to contemplate how that affects the legal status of our marriage. Bonnie's mother had her wedding dress made for her, and Bonnie *hated* it. She also *hated* having the reception at her parents' country club with all of *their* friends and none of *ours*. For all I knew Bonnie might already have hated *me*. We were off to a flying start.

And we still had to get rid of Irene in order to start our lives together. The woman who had kept her ear to the ground and who tore through the papers looking for opportunities for her kid was still treating me like a kid—expecting me and my wife to live our lives according to her plans. There were the constant phone calls, the constant demands for our time, and the asking for more money. I had to make her understand that I was now a married man, albeit one with a lot of growing up to do. Ultimately I had to be cruel and literally stop talking to her, but it was the only way to create some kind of separation.

This meant Irene could now turn her whole attention to my sister Carol, who was still only a teen. Carol was at the High School of Performing Arts. This was a bad idea since it was all about performing, something she really didn't want to do. She simply cut classes and dropped out of school all together. Carol had one of the best agents in New York, Jane Broder, who had arranged an appointment for her with F. Hugh Herbert, author of the big comedy hits *The Moon Is Blue* and *Kiss and Tell*. Carol resisted going to the appointment, but Irene insisted. Carol agreed to go "if Billy goes with me." So off we went to Mr. Herbert's suite in a New York hotel. Once we got there Carol asked to speak to me privately.

"I'm sorry, Mr. Herbert, but would you mind going into the other room?" I asked.

He took himself off to the bedroom.

"Billy, I'm too scared. I'm just scared." She started to cry.

I wasn't going to put my sister through this. I just wasn't, so when Mr. Herbert returned I said, "I'm sorry, Mr. Herbert, but she won't read. She's just too scared. She doesn't want to do it." With that, Carol and I started to move toward the door.

"You don't understand," Mr. Herbert said. "I'm really interested in her."

I turned back toward him and gave him an apologetic smile. "Well, she doesn't want to do it. She's just too scared."

And we were gone.

Carol was obviously a talented actress. She had that husky singing voice, as well as good looks, and she had been able to hold the stage with Walter Huston, who loved playing scenes with her. She could attract the attention of a top agent, something I hadn't been able to do.

I wonder if I should have behaved differently on that morning with Mr. Herbert. Maybe I should have tried to explain to Carol that there was nothing to be afraid of; it was just an audition. *Carol had never had to audition for anything before.* She had been pushed to do things that frightened her since she was three years old. Irene would have pushed her through the audition, but I simply couldn't. Carol had at that point many years of performing behind her, and it still scared her. She just didn't have the constitution for it and certainly not the ambition. As we closed the door on Mr. Herbert's suite that day, we were closing the door on Carol's acting career. She never performed on Broadway again, though she still sang on *The Horn & Hardart Children's Hour.* My mother was furious with me.

My mother always thought that it would be my sisters who would have longtime careers—my mother considered me a good dancer, but she believed that it was the girls who had the true star potential; they really had the personality and the singing voices. She felt obligated to push them, and as a result she pushed too hard.

The years that followed were very tough for me. Bonnie supported us doing odd jobs. She was a saleswoman at Saks Fifth Avenue and Bloomingdale's and a secretary to a dermatologist. I seemed incapable of doing anything.

Early on I tried being a counter-man at a diner in Hempstead, Long Island. My father had purchased it with money my sister and I had earned doing a radio show, and he had also invested in it the $7,000 I had given him—money I had earned in the army. There would be no salary for me; I would be working for tips. So there I was, standing behind the counter, wearing a white jacket and a little white paper hat, taking customers' orders, handing the order slips to the cooks, and serving up the plates of food. After working seven hours that first day I came home with my "tips"; I should say "tip," because what I took out of my jacket was a dime. That's right, ten cents. It was probably all that I deserved, considering my bad attitude, but I knew then and there I wasn't meant to wait on people.

Granted, there were some orders that I found rather unusual, like the guy who ordered four scrambled eggs sautéed in ketchup. A look of disgust may have flashed across my face, but only for the briefest of moments. Surely the customer, with his nose in the menu, couldn't have noticed my grimace. Perhaps I shouldn't have said, "You want what?"

The customer's look was enough to tell me that my question hadn't gone over very well. I resigned the next day.

As hard as it may be to believe, in the 1950s you could live on one hundred dollars a month in New York City. We lived in a five-floor walk-up on East Sixty-Ninth Street for sixty-nine dollars a month. And as for food, you could buy a fish dinner for only a buck. So we were able to get by with odd jobs.

Bonnie and I took a night shift at a bank in lower Manhattan, she doing something respectable like typing and I, unable to type, doing something menial like filing, since I did know the alphabet. Going home in an empty subway car in the wee hours of the morning, I turned to her and said, "I'm not going back there ever again."

"Neither am I," she said.

A friend of ours got me a job at a mail-order house—Reuben H. Donnelly. The only memorable moment was when a vigilant coworker called us all to the windows facing the Beaux Arts Hotel and Apartments, where a "lady of the night" working the day shift had ushered her client into the bedroom and neglected to pull the blinds. She proceeded to service her customer in full view of the hooting and howling employees of Reuben H. Donnelly.

Finally there was *Mister Peepers*, a half-hour live TV comedy show on NBC starring the comedian Wally Cox. Georgann Johnson, a friend of ours from Northwestern who was appearing on the show, got me a job. I was to sit in the middle of the audience and start the laughs. When a line came along that I thought was funny or I thought the writers thought was funny, I'd give a guffaw—a guffaw that erupted from me in such a way as to seem irrepressible. That would get the audience started, and if they seemed reluctant or uncertain I might continue on, slapping my leg and laughing like a maniac. For this I got twenty-five dollars, which in those days was nothing to sneeze at—or laugh at, for that matter.

"Making the rounds" was the ritual that actors followed in trying to get a foothold in theater or television in New York. This consisted of visiting offices—of agents, when seeking representation, or casting agents, when seeking a job—or listening for scuttlebutt wherever actors hung out.

This is where my uncertainty and ambivalence about being an actor kicked in, for I was unable to practice any of these routines with any sort of consistency. I was unable to schmooze with or sell myself to the few agents I got to see. With no agent representing me, I would arrive at a casting agent's office without an appointment, give my name to the secretary, sit down, and wait to be seen. When it became obvious that I wasn't going to be seen, I'd leave, having given the secretary a photo that I'm sure wound up in the wastepaper basket next to her desk.

I spent a lot of time escaping to double features at movie theaters, and so did Bonnie. While she was doing her various odd jobs, I spent hours listening to music at Sam Goody's and visiting art galleries. It was, I guess, an education. It filled up the days.

At home my inertia was no laughing matter. It baffled Bonnie and worried her. I'm sure she came to think our marriage was a mistake.

I didn't even ponder my future. I just sat—in a fog. It never occurred to me at the time that, other than taking Howard Lindsay's suggestion that I go to college, serving in the army for two years, and studying for three and a half years at Northwestern, my life had been directed and managed by Irene. I had rarely initiated anything myself. However, when I'd been asked to do something, I had always performed well.

And now I was left with little desire, no initiative, and no ambition.

In 1951 I got a job as a supernumerary (an extra with no lines) in a Margaret Webster revival of Shakespeare's *Richard II* starring Maurice Evans. As a page, I entered with a message for the king, knelt on one knee before him, and tried to dodge the spittle propelled by his mellifluous voice.

I don't seem to remember any of the good reviews I may have received over the years, but I do remember the bad ones. One particularly memorable one was when I was cast as Sub-Lieutenant Grainger in the Theatre Guild's production of a British import called *Seagulls Over Sorrento*. It had been a big hit in London but not so in

New York in 1952, even with a cast that included Rod Steiger, Leslie Nielsen, Mark Rydell, and John Randolph. In the second act I entered and said one of my very few lines: "This is it, men!"

Wolcott Gibbs, the theater critic for the *New Yorker*, wrote in his review, "When Sub-lieutenant Grainger entered and said, 'This is it, men!,' I agreed with him and left the theater."

The line was taken away from me the next evening, which happened to be the last evening of our New York run.

In 1953 I was hired by a summer stock company for a nine-week season, playing split weeks in Easthampton and Westhampton in Long Island. Bonnie did secretarial work for the producer of the theater, Ron Rawson, and then replaced the ingénue when she quit. Nine plays in nine weeks! The thought of having to do it now boggles the mind. But we were both young and being paid what amounted to a respectable single salary (when you put our two salaries together).

It was a decent group of plays, one that included Arthur Miller's *The Man Who Had All the Luck*, his first Broadway play, which had closed after only a handful of performances, and *Ladies in Retirement*, in which I played a young killer. And then there was the English comedy-mystery *The Bishop Misbehaves*, in which I played what was called in those days the juvenile lead. The starring role of course was the bishop. The well-known British actor Leo G. Carroll had consented to play the part, and he flew in from California, where he was on hiatus from the successful television series *Topper*.

Mr. Carroll was a gifted actor and a charming man, witty and courteous, with a courtly manner. But he arrived at the first rehearsal having memorized only part of the first act, and as the week's rehearsal progressed he seemed to lose track of even that. He later confessed to me that when he had taken the job he thought he had once played the role somewhere. He couldn't remember where. But when he sat down in the plane and opened his copy of the play, he quickly realized that he had never played the part nor indeed had he ever seen the play. As the week went on apprehensions grew among the cast and the director. And since there were just six days of rehearsal in summer stock, which included a final day of technical run-through, and Mr. Carroll was being cued his lines through all of these rehearsals, the anxiety among the cast grew palpable. Mind you, we in the cast were also performing another play in the evenings. So it was wisely decided that Mr. Carroll should have at his disposal prompters upstage left, downstage left, upstage right, and downstage right—four young apprentices in the wings with scripts at the ready.

On opening night I, the juvenile, and Ann Hillary, the ingénue, played our opening scene into which Mr. Carroll made his first appearance. He entered from stage left, and when the audience applauded, he stopped, looked out at them, and said, "Oh, thank you very much."

Oh Lord, we were in for some evening. Our scenes were almost entirely with the bishop, and quite often we would throw him a line and wait while he stared at us. Then he would say something like, "Oh dear, well there we are, now let me see," as he wandered upstage to be cued by a frightened young apprentice and then wandered back, mumbling, to center stage to give us the long-awaited reply.

This went on all evening. At one point Mr. Carroll shuffled upstage to get a line, which the apprentice whispered to him. He looked toward her and said, "I beg your pardon?" The poor girl, stunned, repeated the line loudly enough to be heard in the back row.

As far as I know, none of the audience left the theater during the play that evening; perhaps they were fascinated by what appeared to be an improvised performance. The climax of this tragic evening came in the middle of the last act, when Ann and I were having a scene with the bishop and in the middle of the scene he suddenly said, "Oh, there's the doorbell." Of course there was no doorbell, but he proceeded upstage right to the door. We hadn't finished our scene, but before I could think of anything to say to stop him, he opened the door and there stood the three wide-eyed and frightened crooks who knew they were not supposed to enter yet.

"Come in, come in," the bishop said. So, stiff-legged, the crooks shuffled in until the bishop turned and saw the ingénue and the juvenile whom these fellows were never supposed to meet.

"Oh dear," said Mr. Carroll. Recovering, he said, "Now I would like you young people to wait in my study while I deal with these chaps." Yet another improvisation. He led us off stage left, though we had never completed our scene with him.

At the end of the evening I was waiting for Leo in my rented car to take him out for a bite to eat. I now called him Leo, since we shared a dressing room, one in which, among other interesting things, he showed me how he applied his eye makeup. He placed a dime over his closed eye and drew a circle around it, in red! I didn't know if he was kidding or not. But come to think of it, with his face it really didn't matter. He got into the car.

"Where to?" I asked.

"To the nearest state line," he said.

We wound up in a diner outside of town, the kind of place that's built as an imitation railroad car. It had a long counter and some booths, and on the counter stood a huge bowl of eggs, probably for decorative as well as practical purposes.

As he sat down in a booth Leo said, "You know, I have been across this country many times, in planes, trains, and even cars, but I have never come across the army of chickens that it must have taken to create all the eggs that you seem to have here"—an observation that was perhaps inspired by the egg he had laid that night.

So from 1951 (the year Bonnie and I got married) to 1959 I was in bad shape mentally because of my nonexistent career. Oh, I occasionally got a role, in dramatic TV shows like those for *Kraft Playhouse* or *Philco Playhouse* or *Somerset Maugham Presents* (this was the 1950s and they were broadcast live, an exciting time). But I never got an agent, and I certainly never made a living wage.

One show I remember in particular was an episode of *Somerset Maugham Presents*. I played a tennis pro who, along with his tennis partner (played by Jack Lemmon, who was much in demand as a TV actor but was not yet the movie star he was destined to become), was playing in a tournament on the French Riviera, where they bumped into two French femme fatales.

My date in the script was the 1940s film noir siren Veronica Lake (famous for the hairdo that always covered one eye). She had just walked out on a Hollywood contract and had unwisely agreed to play a fairly large part in a live one-hour network television show.

You got only a week of rehearsals for these hour-long shows in those days. It was something she had never done before, and something she was totally unprepared to do. So she hit the bottle. One day someone had to go to her hotel and escort her to rehearse a ballroom dancing scene we had together, and I could smell the gin. No one at the top seemed inclined to replace her, so we went live from Studio 3A at NBC in Rockefeller Center.

In that same dancing scene Ms. Lake went up—totally dried up—not a word of dialogue out of her. The control room needed certain lines to be spoken that would cue the cameras so they could cut from us to Jack and his date at a ringside table and then cut back and forth between the two couples. But only silence from Ms. Lake. I tried speaking Ms. Lake's lines in the form of a question so I could answer the question I had just asked. In there somewhere were cues for the control room, but I must have sounded demented. This went out to the whole country.

Later Jack consoled me, saying he had run into the same thing on other shows that imported unemployed Hollywood actresses. But one good turn does *not* deserve another. Ring Lardner Jr., critic for the *New York Post*, in his review of the show seemed fascinated with Ms. Lake (maybe it was the hair), but he lambasted me. I laughed when I read it. I had to; otherwise I might have cried.

It was Bonnie who got the first big break. She was only four years out of school when Dan Petrie, a successful director who remembered her from Northwestern, recommended her for a leading role in a soap opera called *Love of Life*. She beat out a number of more experienced and prominent actresses and after many auditions got the part. She played Vanessa, the starring role, for more than three years and basically supported us while saving money to pay for her analysis—where she sorted things out for several years and probably tried to figure out why the hell she'd married me.

The first hurdle Bonnie had to deal with was that the soap opera was done live and went out over the CBS network live: no taping, no stopping to do retakes. Whatever happened—flubbed lines, actors drying up on their lines, stumbles and fumbles—went out live at noon for all the viewers to see. Since she was the star of the show and all the story lines revolved around her, she carried most of the dialogue. *Love of Life* started as a fifteen-minute show airing five times a week, but for the last year and a half that Bonnie was on it, *Love of Life* was a half-hour show. Memorizing lines day in and day out became a nightmare for Bonnie. She would lie in bed, script on her lap, trembling and awake half the night at the thought of having to go back into that studio again. I sometimes cued her on her lines, sometimes held her in my arms, and sometimes would say, "Oh honey, I wish I could go in there and do the scene for you."

During the years before *Love of Life* (and after), we studied acting in Lee Strasberg's private acting classes. Actually Bonnie studied there, and I just tagged along to keep track of the guys with whom she was doing scenes. She quickly became a favorite of Lee's and was appointed his class secretary in charge of collecting students' fees and assigning scenes.

Strasberg was the guru of the famous Actors Studio and a leading proponent of Stanislavsky's acting method. Once again I half-assedly backed into something good when I got involved in that class. Bonnie paid my fees.

I think I endorsed the idea that you couldn't teach acting; you had to "learn it on the boards," a nineteenth-century notion that I probably got from an old character actor in *Life with Father* by the name of A. H. Van Buren, a name that belongs right up there with Edwin Booth. "Learning it on the boards" simply means learning to act on an actual stage in an actual theater. I resisted the idea that there were "boards" on the little stage of the Malin Studio, where Lee taught his classes, and that you could learn about acting there. I think Lee sensed this attitude. Once when he asked the class to critique a scene I piped up to say that it had lacked pace. He hit the roof—pace was not what Strasberg was looking for. And when I got up there on that little stage, he destroyed me.

"When I look at you, as a director, I wouldn't know what to do with you. I don't know who you are," he said.

He meant that he didn't know who I was behind the façade I put on and called acting.

When I auditioned at the Actors Studio and failed, Lee asked Bonnie how I thought the audition had gone.

"He thought it went all right," she told him.

"It was a cheap imitation of Robert Montgomery," Lee said.

I didn't think Montgomery was such a bad actor, but Lee got to me; he punctured the little self-confidence I had. But little by little, without even thinking about it, almost by osmosis—I began to change. And things began to change for me.

Now looking back on it perhaps I can put into words the things that went into that change in my acting. Remember, my sisters and I were a song-and-dance team. We'd get out there jigging and singing away with lots of energy and smiles plastered on our faces—we were entertainers. Entertaining is not acting. But it's what I attempted to bring to my acting, and it was all superficial. For instance, Strasberg had a "song" exercise in which you were to stand straight and still and simply sing a song. It was an attempt to take away all your mannerisms, your attempts to "sell" the song. But I didn't stand still on the stage. I sat on the apron and sang "Making Whoopee," trying to get a laugh, trying to entertain, but missing the whole point of the exercise or, to be honest, openly rejecting it.

That's what brought out Lee's sharp remarks. *"I wouldn't know what to do with you. I don't know who you are."*

I began to slowly drop all that. There was a point to that exercise, an important point. When you take on a role, you should ideally start with nothing—no mannerisms, no preconceived ideas of how things should go—just leaving yourself open to where the part will take you. It takes a certain amount of courage, and you're of course restricted by what the play demands—that certain things should happen and certain staging should take place. But within that context you try to leave yourself open to whatever emotions, urgings, or impulses the lines of dialogue bring out of you. What you're looking for is spontaneity and colors in your performance that might surprise even *you* and might even change, if only slightly, your performance from one night to another. And finally this approach can allow you to present, in any role, who you are: what constitutes your humanity, your sensibilities, your wit (if you have any), and the well

71

within you that contains your fears, your hopes, and your shames. From this well you can pick and choose the things that are appropriate for your role in the play, and it's what talented actors bring to a performance. The true art of an actor is remaining unprepared even in the rehearsal and blocked-out scenes of a play but prepared to meet it, moment by moment, with all that one has observed and accumulated of life's experiences.

The turning point came in class one day when Bonnie and I did a portion of *From Here to Eternity*, and for the first time I was comfortable in my own skin, playing someone else but allowing the human being inside me to come through.

The changes that took place in me were in no small measure due to the fact that Bonnie and I became friendly with and almost part of the Strasberg family. Bonnie, as Lee's class secretary, led the way, and I followed her into their family circle. The Strasbergs held a European-style Sunday soirée where you might come across just about anyone prominent in New York's theatrical circle, as well as refugees from Hollywood, starting with Marilyn Monroe.

In person without makeup Marilyn was pretty ordinary looking. She had magnificent eyes but none of the Hollywood blond-bombshell look. In fact her hair was curly and reddish at the roots, and her cheeks were always ruddy. She was a great comedienne and gave us a glimpse of her dramatic talents when she gave a poetic and moving performance in a scene from *A Streetcar Named Desire*. She did the scene where Blanche says to the delivery boy, "Young man! Young, young, young man! Has anyone ever told you that you look like a young prince out of the Arabian Nights?!" I also remember in that scene she was sweating profusely, from every part of her body—she must have been terrified.

She was always striving to better herself, both as an actress and as a person. Once in Strasberg's kitchen she walked up behind Bonnie, who was having an intense conversation about the art of theater with director Walter Beakel, and she said, "I want to feel what it's like to be talked to like an intelligent person."

We became regulars on Sunday afternoons at the Strasberg apartment on the Upper West Side; in fact eventually I felt we were *expected* to show up. Sometimes it was just Bonnie and I and Lee's family—his wife Paula and his children, Susan and Johnny. I can remember sitting around the kitchen table having a snack, with Lee serving tea and maybe a bagel. That was the strange thing about this man: you could barely get a word out of him, and yet in the kitchen he could be so low key and gracious as he served you tea.

Often, whether just the family was there or there was a crowd, Strasberg would wander off into his study to listen to music and I'd follow him. The ceilings in his study must have been twelve feet high, and one whole wall contained shelves, floor to ceiling, stacked with classical records. It looked like Sam Goody's record shop, of which Lee was a valued customer. He'd put an LP on the turntable, sit back in his easy chair, and listen for a few minutes. Then he'd get up and change it to a new recording, maybe one he'd just bought. I remember I was enjoying a recording so much that when he started to change it I said, "Hey, let's listen to the rest of it."

Lee just waved his hand in dismissal and put on a new piece of music. There was never a word exchanged between us in those listening sessions, and yet I know that if he didn't want me there he would have let me know, if not with words then with the Lee Strasberg stare.

It was during this period that I began to take Lee's classes seriously. I came to know that if you put aside the lectures, the criticisms, and the silences, Lee was a kind and generous man who knew what he was talking about when it came to acting. And in later years when he came backstage after having seen a performance of *The Zoo Story* and complimented me on my work, I floated out of the theater. Other than those few complimentary words and a few mumbled responses, I don't ever remember having had a conversation with him.

But the Strasbergs showed their affection for us in many ways. One summer they lent us their lovely home on Fire Island for a week when they knew it was the only vacation we could possibly afford.

I know that Lee Strasberg made me a better actor than I ever would have been without him.

As I mentioned, Bonnie had used her income from *Love of Life* to pay for her psychoanalysis, but she was also paying for mine. I only did this for a few months, and the results were fast and lasting. Our marriage was in big trouble at the time because my self-esteem as an actor was near its lowest; together and separately we were in need of repair. The main thing I learned was that I couldn't control everything—that I needed to just let things happen and play themselves out. Because I was constantly trying to control Bonnie, she wanted out of the marriage. There was even one night when I packed my bags and walked out. I didn't get very far, however, and returned to say that the books and records in the apartment were mine and if she really wanted "out" she would have to be the one to go. She said "okay" and then went back to bed. (I wouldn't go back into therapy until I started working on this book.)

Unfortunately, telling others that you are in analysis makes you vulnerable—especially to those who would like to make you their "patsy."

Herbert Berghof was a well-known actor, director, teacher, and founder of the Herbert Berghof Studio, where many an actor got training. I wasn't one of them. I unfortunately came across him in his least-practiced profession, as a director. I remember being interviewed by him in his Washington Square home that he shared with his wife and teaching partner, the wonderful actress Uta Hagen. He was casting Shakespeare's *Twelfth Night*, which he was to direct at the Cambridge Drama Festival. He had already assembled quite a cast, which included Tammy Grimes, Fritz Weaver, and the Irish star Siobhan McKenna. Ms. McKenna was to play Viola, and Berghof was considering me to play her twin brother, Sebastian, but unfortunately during the interview I mentioned that I was in psychoanalysis. I told him that I was sure I could take leave of it for this production, even though my analyst was against my leaving at that point. Berghof never forgot I'd revealed that I was in analysis and probably assumed I was in a fragile state, which I was not.

It has been my experience that insecure directors, for whatever reason (lack of experience or of confidence in their talent or uncertainty as to how to handle a production) are wary of giving direction to their prominent players or stars, so they look for someone else to badger, a patsy they can criticize with impunity. In front of the whole cast Herbert excoriated my performance to the point that Tammy Grimes had to speak up and say, "Oh, Herbert, please." That seemed to pull him up short. It should be noted that I was giving a good performance. In fact Tammy's husband at the time came over and complimented me, saying that what I was doing was the proper style for Shakespeare. Tammy's husband was Christopher Plummer, the Canadian star and Shakespeare specialist. At any rate, that freed me from being Herbert's patsy, and I never allowed him to say another word to me.

In 1956 I had a phone call from our friend George Segal, who said he was being drafted into the army. He wanted to know if I'd be interested in replacing him in the role of Don Parritt in the José Quintero production of *The Iceman Cometh* by Eugene O'Neill, which was playing Off-Broadway at the Circle in the Square Theatre. Although the salary was minuscule (would you believe forty-five dollars a week?) and it was a hugely unsympathetic role (I'm sure O'Neill hated the kid), it was a long-running, successful production that I think did a lot to establish Circle in the Square Theatre and Off-Broadway, as well as "downtown" as a place that people were willing to travel to and visit. Besides, I needed an acting job, and meeting the famous José Quintero might be beneficial to my career, so I took the job. I never did meet Mr. Quintero. He never came to the theater to check his production, as most directors do when they pop in to make sure the show is still tight and on course.

I was rehearsed by the stage manager for a week, and he just held the script and ran my dialogue with me. I never had a full rehearsal with the cast, which is crucial, especially in an almost four-hour play like this one. An actor needs to see and hear what transpires before and after his dialogue. My opening night was a nightmare because there were lengthy scenes before I spoke, and I didn't always know when my dialogue was to occur. I shared a little dressing room with the Viennese actor Paul Andor, who played an old drunk in the play, and on my opening night as I nervously applied my makeup he turned to me and said, "Bill, you know that place in the third act where you come and sit at my little table?"

"Huh? Yeah, I think so," I said.

"Well, it's so long and I sit there with my arms and head on the table. I sometimes fall asleep, so before my little speech would you give me a little poke with your elbow?"

"Poke you? Poke you? Are you out of your mind? I barely know when *I'm* to speak. And you want me to nudge you before *you* speak?"

I was practically screaming at the poor guy. He held up both his hands as if to ward off an expectant blow.

"All right. All right," he whispered. "Of course, forgive me. You have your own problems."

Also in the cast was the wonderful actress Eileen Ryan, who was married to actor Leo Penn (later to become a very successful TV director). Leo, by the way, took over the lead in the play toward the end of the run. Leo and Eileen were longtime friends and would become the parents of Sean Penn, who as we all know has had an extraordinary career.

I didn't last long in *Ice Man*. The production was in such poor shape, and without a director's attention over such a long run the tempo of the show was reduced to a snail's pace, with the actors indulging themselves in such over-the-top acting that I just walked away from it. After three months I turned in my two weeks' notice.

But the most important event for me as an actor in the 1950s was when I auditioned for the role of Brick Pollitt in the national touring company of Tennessee Williams's *Cat on a Hot Tin Roof*. After I finished my audition the director came up on the stage and said, "Bill, you're really a fine actor and I look forward to working with you in the future, but for this part you just don't look like a football halfback."

I had spent most of the past decade being rejected by theater companies such as Williamstown and others. So fine. Here was another one. I went home and forgot about it. A week or two passed and I got a call to come back and audition again. It seems that Tennessee Williams and his agent, Audrey Woods, had cast approval for this company and didn't like the director's choice for the roles of Brick and Maggie, the two leading parts.

I went back and read for the role again. This time Tennessee

Williams chose me for Brick and Olga Bellin for Maggie. *Tennessee Williams chose me.* I can't tell you what that meant to me, to my sense of worth as an actor, to a career that I sometimes felt like I'd stumbled into.

The director who had rejected me proved to be of no help with my performance. The experience taught me to listen to directors with one ear but use the other ear to listen to the inner voice that is telling me how to play the role. It's not that I don't trust directors. They stage the play. They tell you where to stand and when to sit (if I agree). But I don't believe I've ever listened to one who started giving me line readings. The worst directors I've run into have never been actors. They can pull all the elements of production together—scenery, lighting, costumes, and casting—but only a director who has been an actor understands how to give acting notes to a performer.

Cat on a Hot Tin Roof was a nine-month, cross-country tour. (Again, my analyst had advised me not to take the job—he didn't think my marriage would survive that long a separation.) Week-long stands in major cities and some split weeks in smaller towns. Thirty-three weeks of eight performances a week and then, on Sunday, your day off, traveling to the next town. It was a long time to be away from Bonnie. She visited me occasionally, but she was busy doing five days a week on *Love of Life*, as well as understudying in a Broadway play. Surprisingly our marriage survived. Obviously we wanted it to.

One incident stands out from that tour. It happened in Florida.

When we hit Coral Gables to open on a Monday night, there wasn't much time to work out any glitches, and as it happened there was a big one. The management of the Coconut Grove Playhouse informed Victor Jory, who was playing Big Daddy, that the black actor playing the servant would not be allowed to perform.

We'd had an afternoon rehearsal, so word of this glitch didn't reach Victor until he was sitting in his dressing room at the half hour, applying his makeup. A sold-out house was filling up with people taking their seats.

"If he's not allowed to perform, the show does not go on," Victor said. And so the ruckus began. The management claimed precedents. No black actor had ever been allowed to perform at that theater, and they saw no reason to change the policy for us. The audience sat patiently waiting. Victor was adamant. Finally permission was granted. But that wasn't really the end of it since the black actor couldn't find a hotel that would allow him to stay. The man ended up staying with a black family who, on opening night, invited the cast to their home for coffee and cake. Behind the house was a long alley, where we parked our rented cars. It was a pleasant but short visit, and when we went out back to retrieve our cars, both ends of the alley were blocked by police cruisers, spotlights shining in our direction. Our little cast stood dumbfounded as the officers slowly walked toward us.

"What are you all doing in there?" one of them asked.

"We're the cast of *Cat on a Hot Tin Roof*," Victor said. "We're playing at the Coconut Grove Playhouse. So, if you're going to arrest us, you'd better let the theater know that there won't be a performance tomorrow night."

Total silence from the police. They looked us up and down. The one who seemed to be in charge said, "You're in the wrong part of town, so get in your cars and get out of here."

We were glad when our week in Coral Gables was over.

When I got back to New York, I got a chance to do the show again, this time in Connecticut with Diana Barrymore, the daughter of the legendary Shakespearean actor and movie star John Barrymore. Both John and Diana had tragic personal lives and died young. Diana, like her father, was talented but a complete mess. When I arrived at her hotel room, her manager, who was a woman, invited me into the bedroom to meet Diana—then promptly left us alone there. The first thing Diana said to me was, "You should oil your body for the part." I excused myself, went to the theater management, and gave my two-week notice (which meant that I still had to rehearse and open the play with Diana). Bonnie said it was the best first act of that play she'd ever seen because my contempt for my leading lady was so frighteningly real.

In November 1958 I played Jimmy Porter in *Look Back in Anger* at the Forty-First Street Theatre. That theater was considered Off-Broadway, but many people in the business came to see the play.

I did not listen to the director in that production either. I don't remember the circumstances that led to our mutual dislike—perhaps it was line readings—but I was on my own when it came to interpreting this role. And quite a challenge it was. A good experience for me. Jimmy was very verbal, very quixotic, very erudite—and with a British accent! I look back—not in anger—but with fond memories. I was about to get my big break, and thanks to all my experiences—both the good and the bad—I was ready for it.

7

I've Been to the Zoo

My big break almost didn't happen. Up until the late 1950s, from early childhood on, my life had been a kind of a nonstop acquiescence. While it was true that I had quit a couple of productions and ignored a few directors, I had really never said no to acting opportunities. During the early New York years I took every job I could get my hands on.

I had stepped in to save my sister Carol with the word *no*, but I was only advocating for someone else. When I finally decided to say it for myself, it was (almost) the biggest mistake of my life.

In 1959 I got my first big break in New York. Director Milton Katselas was familiar with my work in Strasberg's class and asked me to read for a play he was directing Off-Broadway. It was Edward Albee's first play to be produced in New York, a one-acter called *The Zoo Story*. It was to be presented on a double bill with the New York premiere of Samuel Beckett's *Krapp's Last Tape*, a one-character drama. Beckett was of course the author of *Waiting for Godot*, which had been presented on Broadway a few years earlier, and "the latest Beckett play" was anticipated to be a hot ticket. Even though the Beckett play was to be first on the bill, it wasn't a "curtain raiser." *The Zoo Story* in fact was considered to be of less importance. Until it hit the stage, that is.

It was a two-character play in which one character, Jerry, did most of the talking and the other character, Peter, mostly sat and listened. I was not impressed with the play; it seemed wordy and out of balance. It wasn't the first play I misjudged, and it wouldn't be the last. But I went to the audition in this little theater called the Provincetown Playhouse (yes, the place that Eugene O'Neill made famous, not that I knew it at the time) and assumed I would be reading for the big part—after all, it was Off-Broadway, and I'd played the lead in a national touring company of a Broadway show. They let me read a couple of Jerry's lines, stopped me, and asked me to read Peter, the listener.

I could tell, I could just feel that they liked what they heard, and I thought, *Oh boy, they're gonna offer me this little part.* And they did.

As I've mentioned, I always see what I think are the problems in a role or play. I'm not the kind of actor who says, "Boy, I've got a great part in this great play," when the part isn't great at all. I've heard that often enough. My inclination was to turn down such a small part.

Our dear friend from college, the director Gerald Freedman, who had seen the play at the Actors Studio, said, "Bill, you've got to do this play. Albee is a new and brilliant playwright." Bonnie agreed that I mustn't turn it down. So, having received my instructions, I took the part. The Actors Studio workshop had featured an older man playing the role of Peter, but Milton thought it would work better if the actors were approximately the same age. So he thought of me.

The rehearsal period was tumultuous. After more than a week of sitting at the rehearsal table reading the play aloud (a very important period in which the actors become accustomed to their roles, feel out their relationships, become aware of the dramatic moments), the producers and, I assume, Edward Albee got nervous about not seeing the actors up on their feet, so they fired the director, Milton Katselas.

Richard Barr, one of the producers, took over the direction and got us on our feet (actually he got me on my bench since I didn't get on my feet until the end of the play). Richard Barr started directing the young and very talented actor playing Jerry, George Maharis.

George had certain qualities that worked very well in this play. He had an ability to be menacing and yet, at the same time, appear vulnerable and needy. He drew you in. Like Brando, he played his role so that you never knew what was coming next, and nothing seemed planned. There was a sense of danger. (Very few people saw George's performance. He left after a couple of weeks to fulfill a commitment to do a TV pilot—for *Route 66*—and never returned to the play. While there were actors who came after him and may have given great performances, none captured George's unique quality, perfect for the role. I'm sure if he had been able to stay with the play, he would have gotten all the awards instead of me.)

In the early rehearsals Barr directed George to move here on this line, there on that line, and over there for that section. None of this was important or had any motivation behind it and was simply mechanical. It made Maharis nervous and upset and rightfully so.

He came to me and said, "If that man continues to direct, I'm going to quit."

"And if he goes, I go," I said to the director.

That brought Katselas back into the picture. He, being young and impetuous—and hurt—said words to this effect: "If anyone comes near me while I direct this play, I'll punch him in the nose."

That caused a breach in the production's staff that never healed. When the play opened and was a success, Milton was barred from entering the theater.

Richard Barr claims in his autobiography to have directed *The Zoo Story*. He did not. Nor did Alan Schneider, who was billed as the director in one of its several revivals. It's been my experience that just about everyone connected to a play will take credit for its success, but few are willing to accept responsibility if it's a failure.

Opening night of *The Zoo Story*, Provincetown Playhouse, 1959:

Actor Donald Davis finishes his performance in *Krapp's Last Tape*, and after the intermission between it and *The Zoo Story* I (as Peter) take the stage and sit on a bench in Central Park, facing my apartment building on Fifth Avenue, reading a book. Jerry (George Maharis) enters stage right, walks in back of the bench, stoops over my left shoulder, and says, "I've been to the zoo."

Without turning to look and see who is speaking, I simply look up—straight ahead—huge laugh! The laugh continues for a long time, and my character is thinking *perhaps the voice is speaking to someone else*, so I almost surreptitiously glance to my right. Another big laugh.

He repeats, "I've been to the zoo."

I'm finally forced to turn and confront him. These laughs were there, every night, wherever we were playing: other playhouses in the Village, in Buffalo, Buenos Aires, and Rio.

In Buenos Aires some of the audience came with Samuel French editions of the play in Spanish. In Rio they brought Portuguese versions. Even where the audience didn't speak English, the laughs were always there and the ovations at the end of the play were memorable.

After the first performance the producers and the director (I'm not sure whether Albee was with them) came rushing backstage to our basement dressing room. They were almost yelling.

"Why are you playing for laughs? This is a serious play."

"I'm not playing for laughs."

"You're looking at the audience!"

"I'm sitting on a bench facing the audience, for Christ's sake. My home is across the street on Fifth Avenue! Do you want me to play the thing looking over my left shoulder and my right shoulder?"

They had no answer for that, and things seemed to subside. The point is that I was as surprised by the laughs as they were. But these weren't your garden-variety comic laughs that are achieved by mugging. These were laughs of *recognition*. The director, the producers, and especially the author should have thanked their lucky stars that those laughs were there because it meant we already had the audience in the palm of our hands. The opening moment of the play—being accosted by a stranger—is something that has either happened to each member of the audience or it's something they fear. This fear lived in the minds of all the audiences wherever we went. It meant that they were looking at this through the eyes of Peter; they identified with him. So I, the *dummkopf*, was playing a very important part, a role for which I received a Village Voice Obie, the Clarence Derwent Award ($500 at a time when I was making $75 a week), and my favorite: in Buenos Aires, I was named "El Actor de habla no Castellana"—Best Actor in a non-Castilian speaking role! I'm not bragging; it's just a testament to the power of this play.

Here is an example of the play's power: I was stopped in Greenwich Village one day by a well-dressed, cultured-looking man in his thirties or forties who turned out to be a professor at NYU.

"I'm very embarrassed," he said. "I hope I didn't make a lot of noise when I left in the middle of the play." There's a part in the play where Jerry tickles Peter mercilessly, and it drove this man right out of the theater. He said, "When he started tickling you, I thought, 'Oh no, this isn't part of the play,' and I kind of ran out. I mean, now I'm going to have to go back to see the end of it. Sorry!"

Here is a bright, educated man who got so caught up in the play he completely lost himself. No actor or play could receive a compliment better than that. By the way, when we first started rehearsing the tickling scene I told Edward Albee that it made me feel uncomfortable. And he said, "That's how you're supposed to feel."

After George Maharis left the show, he was replaced by the actor who was understudying both our parts. While he could have played Peter, he was completely wrong for Jerry. After several weeks of frustration on stage, I went to the producers and suggested my friend Mark Richman (later known more famously as Peter Mark Richman during his long TV career).

With Milton Katselas still banned from the theater, Mark and I had to direct ourselves, going over the staging in my living room. But it all paid off: Mark and I were a smash together for more than a year. It proved to be one of those runs that hit New York every few years, with everyone and anyone who is in show business wanting to buy a ticket. Every night the stage manager would come backstage before curtain and say, "Laurence Olivier is here tonight" or "Joshua Logan is here" or "Elia Kazan."

I played Peter for the better part of two years in all kinds of places; in Rio it was a grand opera house, but there we were on that big stage, just two actors (with Ben Piazza now playing Jerry), a bench, and a trash can. The audience's reaction was incredible; they rushed out of their seats and down to the footlights, applauding and yelling "Bravo!"

We bowed, threw kisses, and shook each others' hands. We even hugged each other. Then we went up to our dressing rooms on a slow freight elevator but were called back to the stage because the audience wouldn't stop applauding.

Edward Albee had written a one-act masterpiece, and it was the beginning of his illustrious career as one of America's greatest and most influential playwrights. And I was lucky enough to have been persuaded by Bonnie and Jerry Freedman to be in it. I had definitely said no, but to no avail. And I also wound up getting an agent out of it. After eight years without one. That's me—backing my way into an almost accidental career.

I have an opinion about all of this, garnered over a long career of not only acting in comedies, straight plays, and musicals but also working on the production team as an assistant director. I am convinced that no one in the creative team that is putting on a stage production (or a film or a television show) knows for sure what he or she is doing.

There's instinct and intuition, there's guesswork, there's past experience, there's luck, but none of it guarantees anything when it comes to making a successful production. You can make or lose a bundle of money; you can make or break a career—it's simply a risky business.

Over and over I've seen the right choices made that led to a success and the wrong choices that led to failure. Among the right choices I've observed: in *1776* an extraneous scene in a whorehouse was cut and a choreographer who was wrong for the job was let go. Among the mistakes: in the musical *On a Clear Day You Can See Forever* the male lead, Louis Jourdan, was replaced and a whole section going back centuries in time was cut (even though, it's true, the play was long). The production had limited success (even with a wonderful score by Burton Lane). It's all guesswork really, even when the guesswork is in the hands of talented people.

Three and a half years after Bonnie began *Love of Life*, by which time she could do the show easily, even with all those lines, both of us decided it was time for her to quit or get a lot more money. (She was being grossly underpaid.) Since she had no agent to represent her, I decided to take matters into my own hands and went to the producer, Roy Winsor, and asked for a substantial raise in Bonnie's salary, almost double. Bonnie felt she deserved it, but she would never be able to ask for it herself. Nevertheless, what the hell was I thinking going in there like that? I wasn't making much money myself (but had had a lot of attention from *The Zoo Story*), and I had never met Roy Winsor. It must have been a first for him—a husband coming in to ask for a raise for his wife. He looked me up and down and said, "You're in a play Off-Broadway, right? How much are you making?" I said, "Seventy-five dollars." He said, "Your wife is already making a thousand dollars a week." He had put me down, but he didn't throw me out; he finished by saying something like, "I'll think it over."

Then he fired her. In my defense I was right to ask for a raise, but looking back, after all these years, I wonder if there was a darker aspect to my actions that I was unaware of—often-unemployed actor living off a busy actress working in a starring role on television, perhaps. Surely I wasn't jealous enough to be that destructive. If I hadn't acted as I did, Bonnie would probably have played in that soap opera for another ten years (her successor in the role did). Bonnie and her talent deserved better than that.

During the "negotiations" Bonnie remembers that the director, Larry Auerbach, told her that they'd love to have her continue at her present salary. She must have wanted off the show or she would have agreed to continue. She was terrified, though, about the loss of income—she was even afraid to spend money on groceries. But I told her, "Don't worry—I'll take care of you." And from that moment on I most certainly did.

Looking back, I think it was at that moment our partnership was stronger than ever—strong enough for both of us to think of starting a family.

After Bonnie left the soap she continued to work in television, Off-Broadway, and regional theaters. But as the new decade began, with both of us in our thirties, our focus was on having children. Finally, in 1962, after working unsuccessfully with doctors for several years, Bonnie suddenly became pregnant just as we had given up.

During her pregnancy I went on a nine-week tour in South America with a repertoire of plays that included *The Zoo Story*. The profit-sharing deal must have lined the pockets of the South American producers, but it produced zero dollars for the American actors.

All that, though, was soon forgotten when Bonnie met me at the airport, all pink-cheeked, full-breasted, and with a bulging belly.

That was about as good as it got, because we then became victims of some bad decisions made by Bonnie's OB/GYN. He allowed her to go a full month past term and refused to induce labor or perform a C-section. The baby boy was born with his lungs full of fecal discharge, and the doctor was unable to clear it. The baby's heart gave out within twenty-four hours. Such a thing would never happen today.

Bonnie, from her hospital bed, was heard to declare, "I'm not leaving this hospital without a baby."

That set us on our path to adoption.

I must confess that the thought of adoption made me uneasy at first, but I figured that since it was Bonnie who had carried our child and gone through the painful birth, it was her call to make. Incidentally, although we never used contraception, Bonnie never became pregnant again.

Initially we applied to a state adoption agency, where we were given a middle-aged woman examiner whose ears pricked up when she heard that (1) we were actors and (2) we'd been in analysis. She required statements from our psychiatrists that led to a long, drawn-out process. In the meantime our friend Georgann Johnson suggested that we contact her OB/GYN, Dr. Norman Pleshette, father of the actor John Pleshette and uncle of Suzanne Pleshette. We did so, and it wasn't long before he called to tell us that he had a fifteen-year-old patient who was expecting a child in three months. She was an out-of-town girl who needed to be put up somewhere near Dr. Pleshette so he could attend her. We never met the birth mother—in those days that simply wasn't done.

We found friends in the suburbs of New York who took the girl in and placed her in one of New York's finest hospitals for the birth of our son. I still had trepidations about the whole adoption thing, but it turns out I had had no reason to worry. Michael David Daniels was born. He was a beautiful, bright-eyed, well-behaved baby—a gift from heaven. That was in 1963, and two years later we lucked out again with the same doctor and the same hospital in another direct adoption. After three days in the hospital Robert Dryden Daniels was ready to come home. I was on the road in *On a Clear Day You Can See Forever*, so my friend Gene Wilder stepped in and acted as my "surrogate" to help Bonnie bring Robert home.

Robert and Michael have been the center of our lives ever since—

two joyous bright lights—and I can't imagine what life would have been without them. After we announced Michael's birth and adoption, we received this note from Edward Albee, who was himself adopted:

JUNE 17, 1963

Dear Bonnie and Bill,

I'm so glad to hear about Michael David. Take very good care of him. Those bumbles can, I'm told and believe, with proper care and love, turn into very nice people.

Fondly,

Edward Albee

8

Sing Out, Louise!

Just before my run in *The Zoo Story* I began a working relationship with the legendary Broadway director Jerome Robbins, one that would last for a number of years. But my first meeting with Jerry was trickier than I could have imagined. Gerald Freedman, my close friend and former college roommate, was assistant director to Robbins, both on the Broadway production of *West Side Story* and on the early rehearsals of the Broadway-bound production of *Gypsy*. I had a phone call from Freedman, who was taking a leave of absence from these rehearsals to direct a television show for David Susskind. Freedman asked if I would be interested in taking over his job while he was away. Since I was unemployed at the time and also interested in directing (I had been doing some directing of scenes at the Actors Studio), I quickly agreed to do it.

For two days I attended rehearsals in the rooftop theater of the New Amsterdam Theatre. (Years ago the Ziegfeld Follies had been presented in the main theater downstairs, and after the show a more risqué version was presented upstairs in the rooftop venue.) Freedman suggested that I come a few days before he had to leave so that he could show me what the job entailed and introduce me to Jerome Robbins, which proved easier said than done. Whenever Freedman began, "Oh Jerry, I'd like you to meet . . . ," Robbins would turn his back on us and walk away.

I didn't know that this was typical behavior from Robbins whenever someone earned his displeasure, which Freedman had done by leaving his job to do a mere television show. On the third day Freedman was gone, and I appeared at rehearsals with sharpened pencils and a yellow pad to take notes on a first-act run-through from a man I hadn't even properly met.

Robbins sat, mid-auditorium, with his sneakers (always sneakers) propped up on the seat in front of him, waiting for the first act to begin. As a sign of deference (I was unwilling to appear too familiar), I put an empty seat between us and sat, pencil poised, at the ready. However, the next moment threw me for a loop. Ethel Merman, starting at the back of the house, came down the aisle shouting, "Sing out, Louise!" to the two little girls who stood onstage; it was just the way my mother had come down the aisle to stand next to me and my sister to get me back on harmony all those years before.

It was like watching my own life unfold, but I didn't have long to dwell on it because I heard a mumble off to my right that surely came from Jerry Robbins.

"I'm sorry, I didn't get that," I said.

Another mumble.

To hell with deference. I moved to the seat next to him.

"I'm sorry, I didn't . . ."

"Tell Marush to forget the rose bit," he said in a very annoyed voice. With the pencil poised above the page I thought, "How the hell do you spell *Marush*? And what the hell is the *rose bit*?"

I could spell everything else, but the words were meaningless to me since I hadn't been to earlier rehearsals. I nevertheless took copious notes.

At one point Ms. Merman was alone onstage speaking to Jack Klugman, who for some reason was offstage answering her.

Without thinking, I said, "That's wrong."

And, without looking at me, Robbins said, "What's wrong?"

"She's standing there with egg on her face. He should be on with her."

Robbins didn't comment. Onstage, with the cast standing around, I recited the notes I'd just taken from Robbins, and he gave them to the actors.

"Next," he said, turning to me, but I'd reached the end.

"That's all there is," I said.

Then Robbins said, "Oh, by the way, Ethel, I'm bringing Jack on sooner at that point. You've got egg on your face otherwise, and also—this is Billy Daniels. Billy, this is Ethel, Jack . . . ," and he went on to introduce me to the whole cast. By God, he *did* know my name.

After Robbins passed on my note to Ms. Merman I was no longer nervous around him. I soon found out there were a lot of people in this production, both cast and staff, who were afraid of Jerry, and for good reason: their livelihoods and careers depended on staying in his good graces. But I was not one of them. My acting career—or what there was of it—lay outside his purview. I didn't speak up often at these rehearsals, but when I did, he listened.

"What is she doing?" I'd say.

"Who?" Robbins asked.

"Marush, upstage left."

"She's stretching, warming up. Getting ready to go on."

"There's a scene going on downstage, and she is being very distracting."

"Well, go tell her to hold it down—face the wall or something." And off I would go.

Jerry was a great artist but a difficult man who would suddenly turn on people for no reason. I remember standing in the back of the house with him in a Philadelphia theater during a run-through, and he suddenly demanded angrily, "What's wrong with this scene?"

"How should I know? *You're* the director."

That shut him up.

As I've mentioned, mistakes are made in every production— some fatal, some not. One mistake: when Jerry was talked into firing a young girl in *Gypsy* who had already worked with him in *West Side Story*. I understood him to be very fond of her, but the composer felt her singing voice was too light for the show.

Then, sight unseen, Jerry accepted the composer's idea for a replacement, a girl recommended to the composer by the director Elia Kazan of all people. (Kazan? In musical theater?) I was sent to New York, along with a pianist and a dance captain, to get her up to speed before bringing her to Philadelphia.

All three of us—pianist, dance captain, and myself—were taken aback by the girl who appeared at the Malin Studio. Her voice was unfortunate; I won't repeat how cruelly it was described later in the reviews. Her acting ability was minimal, and I was not qualified to judge her dancing ability. All I was able to do was make sure she knew her lines. As we got on the train to Philly, I remember telling her that *Gypsy* was a huge production, that Robbins was very busy directing, and that he could be abrupt on occasion. That did nothing to quell the nervousness I could see was already mounting in her. She was, by the way, a very sweet young lady, and it was the composer, Jule Styne, who should have taken the abuse that was handed out to her. (It turned out that Styne had neither seen nor heard her before making the recommendation—what was he thinking?)

We were standing in the back of the theater in Philadelphia when Robbins said, "How is she?"

I could think of nothing to say and simply pointed with my hand as she walked onto the stage. She began to sing.

Styne jumped up from the back of the aisle and yelled, "That's the wrong key! Take it down a key."

But that just lowered the register of a very unpleasant voice. Thank God she remembered the lines we had worked on, but again she said them in that *voice*. Then came the dancing. The short routine ended with a pirouette as she exited. Jerry called her back.

"Do it correctly," he said. She did it again. "You're falling off your turns. Do it again." And she did. "You're falling off again. Do it again." Now he was walking down the aisle, saying, "No, that's not right, again. They told me you could dance! Do it again."

I don't want to exaggerate how many times he made her repeat it. It was many times. And there was silence in the house. No one said, "Jerry, please!"

He was angry at her, at Styne, and at himself. And in the process he destroyed whatever possibility there was for her to improve. She became his patsy. In one actual performance he even hid the batons she needed to make her entrance in one number, forcing her to wiggle her hands with nothing in them as she burst through a scrim.

I relate these events because I was there and witnessed them. I'm neither qualified nor interested in analyzing Robbins's psyche. I can only relate my experiences with him. And many of them were good. The most exciting moments were when I watched his creativity as a director. It goes without saying that he was a giant of American ballet, a choreographer on a par with Balanchine. But he was also a giant in musical theater. Just think of it: *Peter Pan*, *West Side Story*, *Gypsy*, *Fiddler on the Roof*. I can't think of another director of musicals with that kind of record.

While we were in Philadelphia with *Gypsy*, Gerald Freedman, having finished directing his TV show, returned. (Evidently Jerry had forgiven him for leaving.) The day he returned, I stayed home. I thought that was the end of my job, but I got a call from an assistant.

"Jerry wants to speak to you," the assistant said.

Robbins came on the line. "Where are you?" he asked.

"Well, Freedman is back."

"Never mind, I want you back. I need you. See Leland about a salary." (Leland Heyward was the producer.) So I continued my journey with Robbins.

As for the choices that lead to success or failure of a production, hiring a young actress, sight unseen, may have been a mistake, but it wasn't fatal. Not using the ten or twelve chorus girls he had stashed away in a Philadelphia hotel, waiting to be used in a big production finale that never materialized, was a successful choice. Robbins and book writer Arthur Laurents found a simpler and more satisfying ending—"Rose's Turn"—which helped make *Gypsy* a musical classic.

My mother, Irene, came to see the show after it opened, and I wondered if she would recognize herself up there. When I asked her what she thought of Mama Rose, she said, "I think she's a wonderful woman."

In 1963 Robbins asked me to assist him in an Off-Broadway production of a play titled *Oh Dad, Poor Dad, Mamma's Hung You in the Closet and I'm Feeling So Sad*. That's the last time I'll bother to write the full title; henceforth it will be *Oh Dad*. The play is a farce in three acts about a dominating mother who travels to a resort with her stuttering son and her dead husband (in a casket). This time I was Jerry Robbins's only assistant director and was with him from the beginning—and the beginning seemed like an endless period of casting. Perhaps it felt that way because I had to read the other role with each actor who auditioned.

Jerry pumped me for the names of actors we should see, assuming that I was more familiar with the acting community than he was. I believe he liked these long periods of auditioning because hearing various actors read a role gave him an idea of how the role could best be realized. Of course asking actors to re-audition—that is, come back and read again—which he often did, could have unexpected and unfortunate consequences, such as the time a well-known and well-respected actress, Nan Martin, was called back and she appeared with a bottle of champagne and glasses to celebrate her being cast in the part of Madame Rosepettle. It was an awkward moment indeed, and I was the one who had to tell her she was there to audition again, which I tried to do as kindly and respectfully as possible.

It was a crazy play, which I guess you could call a fantasy or theater of the absurd. It could have gone any number of ways and really depended on the actors to pull it off. We were lucky to have Barbara Harris and Austin Pendleton.

Regarding the casting of Pendleton, we were auditioning young men for what seemed like hours to me, probably because I was reading the Barbara Harris role (she was already cast), doing my best to give these young men something to work with as they auditioned to be Madame Rosepettle's shy, nervous, stuttering son. As I led the last of the actors offstage, I saw a young man sitting on the steps with a script in his lap.

"Are you here to read?" I asked.

"Ye—ye-yes," he replied, stuttering as the part required.

"Your name?"

"Au-au-Austin P-P-Pendleton."

Oh come on, I thought, *save that for the reading.*

I didn't have his name on my list of actors, but there he sat, nervous, tentative, with startled eyes behind horn-rimmed glasses, and I thought, *What the hell.* I ushered him on stage.

"This is Austin Pendleton, Jerry. He's not on your list."

Silence from out front, so we started the reading—and for the first time in all our auditions we heard an authentic stutter. Not only that, he never referred to the script. He had it all memorized! And he gave a brilliant, comic reading of the scene. Robbins got up and walked up to the stage.

"That was wonderful," he said. "You've got the part, but I feel like I'm stealing a performance!"

Austin and Barbara were brilliantly funny. We were not so lucky with our leading lady, Academy Award–winning Jo Van Fleet, who, to use a phrase coined by my actor-director friend Stanley Prager, was "as funny as an open grave." I fought against using her, pointing out that she was a formidable dramatic actress but no comedienne. I pushed for a young actress, Zohra Lampert, who gave several hysterically funny auditions, but Jerry deemed her too young for the part. I still believe he was wrong. What the casting of Jo Van Fleet led to was an endless period of rehearsals with Jerry and Van Fleet discussing her character's "inner life." But since her character was one-dimensional, these discussions were a waste of time. These sessions often became edgy, since Van Fleet was a very forceful personality and at times seemed to be usurping the director's job. I remember one moment in the staging when she rose up on the balls of her feet, arms spread wide, and hovered over poor Austin like a witch as she said her lines. Jerry tried to dissuade her from this balletic movement, but to no avail.

"If she does that on opening night, I will stand up and boo," he said. They once had a spat in which Jerry left the rehearsal hall and went downstairs to the cafeteria, where he sat fuming. I had worked previously with Van Fleet in a one-act play by Molly Kazan and was able to talk to her as one actor to another.

"Jo, he's a choreographer. He likes to look at different movements so he can choose. You have to give him that leeway," I said.

She yakked on about an actor's prerogative but finally said, "Okay," and I brought Jerry back with assurances that she'd listen to him. While they had these struggles I often took "the kids," as I called them, Barbara and Austin, into another room to work on their scenes together. They were marvelously inventive and very funny and in fact saved the play.

Jerry came to hate rehearsing with Jo Van Fleet. I remember leaving his townhouse with him, going on foot to the rehearsal hall. As we were crossing Third Avenue Jerry suddenly grabbed my arm and said, "I can't pick up my feet!" I looked down and he was stepping in a pothole that seemed to have just been covered with wet tar; you could see his footprints. I didn't laugh at this because I think he took it as an omen of what lay ahead at the rehearsals.

But the most important and instructive moments for me in this rehearsal period came when, at the producer's urging (or begging), Jerry called in the actors who were to play the hotel waiters (they had been on salary for two weeks without ever being called to rehearse). Jerry planned out the opening scene and turned to the stage manager.

"Tomorrow get me a coffin, a couple of steamer trunks, and lots of suitcases," he said. The stage manager blanched. "All right, they can be cardboard boxes," Jerry added, and the stage manager breathed a sigh of relief.

Jerry also brought in his piano accompanist, who was with him throughout all his productions. At the beginning of the play the five or six hotel waiters were supposed to enter with all this luggage and a coffin (holding poor Dad) followed by Madame Rosepettle and her son. It was quite a crowd suddenly on the stage.

"You're a tough bunch of guys," Jerry said to the actor-waiters as he began directing. "You've probably been playing craps in the basement and were interrupted, called to carry in this stuff."

He turned to the pianist. "Betty, play something bluesy as they enter."

So in they came, a sullen bunch, and dropped the bags wherever they stood. Jerry looked at the scene.

"No, let's forget that. This is a very high-class hotel, and you guys are first-class waiters, very sharp and alert. Betty, play me something upbeat and classy."

In just fifteen minutes he told them where to go, how to carefully place the coffin and luggage, and how to stand at attention as Madame Rosepettle entered. He had them do it three more times with minor adjustments, and it was set. He not only set it, he had put a stamp on the look and style of this play, letting the audience know they were going to be seeing a comedy.

And I thought to myself, *Never mind gabbing with Jo Van Fleet about subtext; this is directing and this is some director!*

On opening night the audience didn't know what to make of the play. The opening scene didn't get any laughs, and Jo Van Fleet was playing what could have been Medea. Not until the second scene, when the kids first meet—with Austin stuttering his lines and Barbara turning her head and delivering her lines to the audience—was there a laugh. The audience suddenly realized it was a comedy. And Jerry and I, sitting in the back of the house, relaxed and realized we were home free. A disclaimer—I don't mean to disparage Ms. Van Fleet; she was a fine dramatic actress. It was simply a case of miscasting, and because of it the play never fully realized its comic potential.

It was another story with the road company of *Oh Dad*, which Robbins had asked me to direct. Van Fleet's role was now being played by Hermione Gingold. Hermione knew a thing or two about comedy, but after she made a grand entrance on the first day of rehearsal it was obvious she was going to be the boss and no one was going to able to direct her. So I quit.

After *Oh Dad* I assisted Jerry again, or I started to assist him, in a Broadway production of Bertolt Brecht's political drama *Mother Courage and Her Children*. The famous play tells the story of a woman who tries to profit from war in the 1600s and winds up losing all three of her children.

There began another lengthy period of auditions, with me onstage reading with the actors. In addition to fielding suggestions from the casting director, Jerry was again pumping me for names of actors I thought might be right for the play.

Past experience had taught me that to mention an actor's name was the kiss of death for that actor. Jerry never cast anyone I suggested; the name had to come from Jerry Robbins himself. One day we were told that Anne Bancroft had arrived to audition and that she had gone into the star's dressing room. She was there to read for the title role of Mother Courage, so we waited for her to appear. I knew Annie from having spent many a Sunday afternoon with her at Lee and Paula Strasberg's soirées, but I had not suggested her for the role, which I suppose improved her chances.

She came onstage dressed in some tattered old rags (where she got them God only knows) that were her idea of what Mother Courage might look like. This kind of enthusiasm from a well-known and well-respected actress must have excited Jerry because he jumped up and suggested that she and I do an improvisation. He'd never suggested anything like that before, and when I heard the situation he set up to improvise, my heart sank.

It went something like this: we're two inmates in an insane asylum who, in the middle of the night, go down to the kitchen to steal food because we're starving, and we fight over the food. I was in no position to object to this absurd notion of his. I could only stare at him and finally submit. And so we commenced to huff and puff on an empty stage without props of any kind. We fought and struggled to find something to say (usually idiotic), and Jerry let this go on for fifteen or twenty minutes. I could have killed him. Not only was it a useless exercise, it had never occurred to him how disrespectful it was. Anne Bancroft was a star of proven abilities and needn't have submitted to this kind of treatment. But Annie very much wanted this role, and by God she got it.

I had been mentioning Maureen Stapleton for the role (to hell with it being the kiss of death; I could just see her doing the part), but she had never responded. Then one day the stage manager came to me and said, "Maureen Stapleton is here. She's in the star's dressing room. She wants to see you."

"Me?"

"Yes."

So I went and knocked on the door, and when I went in Maureen was seated at the dressing table. She turned to me.

"Billy, you keep bringing my name up for this role."

"Yes," I said.

"Billy, I hate this play."

And as soon as she said it I thought, *God, so do I!*

"It was just an idea," I said.

Maureen stood up.

"Thanks, but no thanks." And she was gone.

Shortly after this incident I left the production of *Mother Courage* because I got an offer to play a featured role in a Broadway-bound production starring Gertrude Berg. The show was called *Dear Me, the Sky Is Falling*. I was to receive billing (which I never got as Jerry's assistant) and twice the money I was making, so I jumped at it. (*Mother Courage*, by the way, went on to be one of those legendary Broadway disasters.)

In *Dear Me, the Sky Is Falling* Ms. Berg played a Jewish mother trying to marry off her daughter to someone she thought was a good catch. The daughter accuses her of interfering with her life, and the mother winds up in a psychiatrist's office. I played the psychiatrist. The sight of Ms. Berg stretched out on a couch with a young-looking WASP psychiatrist sitting there, listening to her manipulations, turned into two funny scenes. She was a real pro and very funny doing her shtick in the doctor's office.

Offstage Ms. Berg was kind and thoughtful to me. In fact she gave me permission to leave the show for a week and a half to do a television show in Hollywood. We were in New Haven trying out the play when I asked to be let out; she paused and then said, "You go ahead. But be sure you come back!"

We opened on Broadway to good reviews, and it looked like we were in for a long run. But Ms. Berg became ill, and we soon had to shut down. We were playing at the Mark Hellinger Theatre, and because we had had a huge advance sale they kept the sets in place for months. But Ms. Berg never returned; she died of cancer a few months later.

My final experience with Jerome Robbins came while I was attending the directors unit at the Actors Studio. Our work there consisted of directing scenes or even short plays and presenting them onstage at the studio. I came across a play by María Irene Fornés called *The Office*. It was a strange little play that only lacked an ending. I say strange because there was a foreign flavor to its attitudes and observations of what it was like to work in an office. It was quirky, but I thought it was also very funny. I offered to direct it and proceeded to cast it, put music to it (Berlioz's *Symphonie Fantastique*), and threw a set together. I was very fortunate to get Gene Wilder to take on the leading role. The small cast included Mary Mercier and Mary Sinclair, two wonderful comediennes. It was very well received at the Actors Studio, and the actors began urging me to do it Off-Broadway, but of course it needed an ending. I had no connections with Off-Broadway producers, so I thought to call Jerry Robbins and asked him to produce because I thought, with his name, we could easily raise the money. I told him I wanted to direct it and gave him a description of the play and told him how well it had been received at the Actors Studio. Jerry turned me down, saying he was too busy. I realized it had been a long shot.

Several weeks passed, and I got a call from Gene Wilder saying that Jerry wanted to see the play.

"*The Office?*" I asked.

"Yes."

"You mean he wants you to audition for it?" I asked.

"No, he wants to see what we did with the play. Get on our feet and act it out. Your whole cast."

Jerry, you son of a bitch. But here was my friend Gene Wilder, asking my permission. What could I say? Gene was not a star at that point (that came later), and he was my friend. He and his wife Mary Mercier often played bridge with Bonnie and me. Gene and I played tennis together.

"Well, you can't turn him down, Gene, it's Jerry Robbins! But I'll tell you this: if he does the play, he will never use you. I know him and he will never use my cast," I said.

So that bastard Robbins took the play right out from under me. How did he get hold of the script? How did he find the names of my cast? I never found out. I don't think it occurred to Robbins that what he had done was underhanded. Later I ran into him at a party at Herb Ross and Nora Kaye's apartment. When he saw me, he jumped up from the sofa.

"I found an ending for the play," he said.

"Is that right?" I said. Then I turned around and walked away.

Robbins took the play to Broadway without my cast. Did I indulge in a little schadenfreude when I read the reviews? You bet I did. *The Office* closed after a one-week run. And that was the end of my experiences with Robbins.

I don't want to create a completely unsympathetic portrait of Jerry Robbins—he struck me as a lonely man who spent a lot of time by himself in his East Side brownstone. I remember once he came over to our apartment to play poker, and since he was as awful a poker player as I was, I think he was just looking for friendship.

When I look back on all that time I spent working with Jerry Robbins, I realize those were some of the happiest times I've had in show business. I had breakfast with him at his home when there was rough going with Jo Van Fleet. I would have dinner at his place when we were auditioning actors there in the evening. I was working with a great director and an even greater choreographer. Jerry would move heaven and earth for the success of one of his projects; he would take anything from anywhere or anyone to further his goals. When we were preparing for *Mother Courage* we would sit in his living room listening to Kurt Weill's music and thumbing through photo albums of Brecht's Berliner Ensemble productions. In the end though I think he appreciated me and my contributions. For opening night of *Oh Dad* he wrote this note: "Billy—I don't know if the show is good or bad—but it wasn't possible without you. You have my deep gratitude and devotion always.—J."

I was happy to be a part of it all. So I'm not bitter about what happened with him and *The Office*. It probably never occurred to him that he had taken it away from me. I'm sure he thought that he could do a better job with it than I could—but he was wrong. He certainly should have used my actors.

9

A Thousand and One Clowns

In 1962 I received a call from my new agent, Harriet Kaplan, who had signed me after *The Zoo Story*; I had an appointment to audition for a play that was to star Jason Robards Jr. He was a huge Broadway star at that point, famous for his work in Eugene O'Neill plays such as *The Iceman Cometh* and *Long Day's Journey into Night*.

The play was written by Herb Gardner, best known as a cartoonist, and it was called *A Thousand Clowns*. In the play the character Murray Burns (played by Robards) is a writer who has been unemployed for months after quitting a job he hates: writing for a children's show, *Chuckles the Chipmunk*. Murray is trying to raise his sister's illegitimate son, but social workers (one of them played by me) threaten to take the boy away unless Murray can prove he's a worthy guardian.

It was a strange audition. I was ushered into the basement of the Eugene O'Neill Theatre to find only one other person waiting, a young actress I had never met by the name of Sandy Dennis. In the few words we spoke while waiting, she made it clear that she was already cast in the play and was only there to read with me. It seems I was there at the request of the author, Herb Gardner, whom I'd never met but who had seen me in *The Zoo Story*. That's the way it works in show business. You need to somehow get into a play, be seen in it, remembered for your performance, and seen by a person (an author or director or producer) who just happens to have a play or film or TV series that he thinks you'd be perfect in. At least that's how my career seems to have progressed.

We had a tumultuous rehearsal period for *A Thousand Clowns*. The director, who had been involved from the very beginning of this play, was fired within the first week of rehearsals and the producer,

Fred Coe, took his place. Fred Coe was a well-known television producer, but in my opinion he was not a stage director. He was well liked and never seemed to interfere with what was going on up on the rehearsal stage. He sat in the audience and laughed at Gardner's funny dialogue and enjoyed himself immensely while a group of very talented actors staged the play by themselves. Coe even directed the film version of the play, and a number of scenes later had to be reshot and the whole of it reedited. However, all turned out well in the end. The play was a hit, and the film is still being shown on television, where it holds up very well. But my experience in rehearsals was tough, inasmuch as I had to fight to keep my scenes from being cut. Sometime later Herb thanked me for making my character, Albert Amundson, a human being, since, in his own words, "I wrote the part with you in mind, but I wrote it with a social studies book in my hand." He did, however, write Albert a speech that gave the character an extra dimension—a self-awareness that makes him a believable human being and not a caricature. It was a rather long speech for a comedy, however, and I came to realize that Jason, to whom I was addressing this speech, was uncomfortable just standing there listening, with nothing to do. I felt in my bones that the speech was about to be cut. So I stayed up all night and, with Bonnie's help, made some changes that I thought might save the speech.

At the next rehearsal I told Jason and Fred how I had worked on it. I said I hoped they would take a look at what I came up with.

As originally written, the character played by Sandy Dennis ducks into Murray's closet to avoid me as I enter Murray's apartment. Murray tells me that she's in the closet, but I don't believe him. Then I launch into my speech. I had the idea to open the closet, see her, and close the door again without saying a word. This got a big laugh, but then when I delivered the speech, Jason, as Murray, had something to play with: the awkwardness of her being in the closet and both of us knowing she's there. The speech stayed in the show.

Jason had established himself in dramatic roles such as Hickey in *The Iceman Cometh*, a very serious role in a very heavy O'Neill play (As I mentioned, I was also was in that production, but very briefly and after Jason had left the show.)

Since *A Thousand Clowns* was Jason's first shot at starring in a comedy, I'm sure he felt he needed more help than the current director was giving him. I also think he acted impetuously by firing the first director at the very beginning of rehearsals, and I think he felt guilty about it. I came to this conclusion because, in the second week of rehearsals, he asked me to join him for a drink. I did have one drink with him, but then I excused myself and left him alone in the bar. He disappeared from rehearsals for three days after that.

Herb Gardner came to me at the theater.

"Billy," he said, "you must never leave Jason alone in a bar!"

"How should I know that?"

"If you're with him in a bar, call me before you leave."

Jason finally returned to rehearsals and we proceeded. I do not want to give the impression here that Jason was miscast or not up to playing the part of Murray. He was the main reason that the play was successful. The reality he could create on a stage—the believability of his character's commitment and love for the young nephew he was raising—was the foundation that supported the wit and comedic elements of Herb's play. That time I left Jason alone in the bar led to a special relationship between Herb and me. Sometimes he would share his concerns about Jason's behavior, and later he sought out my impressions of his writing.

Some of Herb's trials and tribulations as Jason's watchdog are funny—sad and funny. Herb had a right to worry. After Saturday night's performances, having finished another eight-a-week, Jason would disappear on a binge. He was married to Lauren "Betty" Bacall at the time (his third marriage and her second, coming after the death of her first husband, Humphrey Bogart). She was the only one who would know his whereabouts. Jason would drink in the Village or on the Lower East Side and end up in a hotel his father used to frequent, which in his father's day was decent enough but was now a flophouse. (Jason Robards Sr. had been a famous actor as well, with a career stretching from Broadway and silent films to television.)

Jason would sometimes resurface Monday afternoon to sleep it off in his dressing room at the theater, but occasionally he wouldn't sober up until the second act of the play, frightening the young child actor who played his nephew. Once, after frantically searching for Jason all night, Herb finally called Betty Bacall and asked if she knew where he might be drinking.

"Have you tried the Village, or maybe that place where the truckers drink on the Lower East Side?" she said.

I suppose the thought of going into that area late at night led Herb to ask, "What'll I do if I find him?"

"Give him a Viking's funeral," Betty snarled, in that signature deep voice of hers.

One night we were at a dinner party at the Robards apartment when Jason wandered in half drunk.

"Good evening, Mrs. Bogart," he said, and he saluted his wife.

That cleared the room.

I spent one night trying to get Jason out of the bar at Frankie & Johnnie's Steakhouse, where he was reciting poetry to a small crowd that had gathered. He was reciting from a book they kept under the bar for his personal use.

I poured him into a taxi, and we made it to his apartment at the Dakota. He pleaded with me to come up for a nightcap because it was his birthday. When I refused, he lay down in the gutter with half his body under the cab.

"Driver, don't move—don't move," I said.

I relented and went up to Jason's apartment with him. As we passed a darkened bedroom a shadowy specter rose up.

"Who the hell is that with you?" Betty roared.

Jason whispered to me, "Shh! Mother Courage!"

I fled the apartment, went down in the elevator, and rushed out onto the street, where the cabbie had wisely waited for me.

The film version of *A Thousand Clowns* was shot in a studio in Hempstead, Long Island. Just before filming began Lee Strasberg had asked me to come to London to do his production of *Three Sisters*, starring George C. Scott, Kim Stanley, and Sandy Dennis. I was flattered that Lee had asked me and most certainly would have said yes if it weren't for the film, which I wanted to do. And so I said no. The play was mercilessly lambasted and the audience literally booed.

The only solace George Scott had was the proximity of his lover, Ava Gardner, who was also in London.

A Thousand Clowns basically takes place in one place (Murray's one-room apartment), so shooting the film should have been simple enough. But it was a problem.

There were cast changes. Gene Saks had played Chuckles in the stage version, but he was unavailable for the film. (Gene would later have a huge career as a Tony Award–winning Broadway director, specializing in Neil Simon's plays.) The role of Chuckles went instead to Paul Richards, and Barbara Harris replaced Sandy Dennis in the cast. Why Sandy was replaced remains a mystery to me, although the word I got was that they were looking for a pretty face. But that didn't make sense since both women were attractive. If I had to guess, I would say that Sandy's whole approach to acting was bothersome to both the author and our leading man. In Boston, Herb Gardner had remarked to me that Sandy could singlehandedly add ten to fifteen minutes to the running time of the play. Perhaps that was an exaggeration, but it was still pretty close to the truth. In her big crying scene while seated next to Murray on his bed, she sniffled, wailed, and stammered and did indeed add minutes to the scene.

Once Jason just stared at her and finally said, "Are you finished?"

She ended her performance by blowing her nose and giving him an innocent look.

Barbara Harris came with her own set of problems. The thought of making her film debut by replacing Sandy Dennis must have scared Barbara to death because she made an extraordinary demand. She wanted to be coached by one Billy Daniels. This demand was met by the producers, and I wound up earning twice as much for my coaching as I made for playing my role in the film.

Since I had worked with Barbara Harris and Austin Pendleton in *Oh Dad*, she evidently trusted me to help her get through *A Thousand Clowns* and her rather large part. I had a great deal of respect for Barbara's acting ability, particularly her gift for comedy. But I also understood what problems might lie ahead when it came to Barbara playing Sandra Markowitz, the social worker who falls in love with Murray.

Barbara came to everyone's attention for her work with The Second City, based in Chicago. The comedy troupe's work was entirely improvisational. They would, for instance, call out to the audience and ask for a topic. Then the actors would instantly improvise a whole sketch based on what they were given. That was Barbara's background; she was most comfortable when she was allowed to go off-script. Learning the lines of a screenplay and sticking to them was another matter. At the Mayflower Hotel on Central Park West we were given a suite where I would urge her to memorize the scenes. I would urge, I would insist, I would demand that she learn the goddamn lines. Barbara would be stretched out on the sofa and, at times, actually doze off.

To get her attention and get her going, I suggested she improvise a scene in which she talks to her mother on the phone and explains why she hadn't communicated recently. Barbara did this brilliantly. She was hilarious. Of course this had nothing to do with the film or her role. When the director and author came to the hotel after their day of shooting to see how we were getting along, I could only say in desperation that we were working on the subtext.

"Barbara, let's show them what we are working on. Let's do that conversation you had with your mother on the phone," I said.

And off she went. She soon had them rolling on the floor.

Perhaps because *A Thousand Clowns* was Fred Coe's first feature film and he was feeling insecure, I was asked not to be on the set to coach her when they filmed the famous crying scene. And that was fine with me. I had my own performance to worry about. Things seemed to go along smoothly. I heard no complaints about Barbara's work. And the shooting finished on schedule.

Months later I was invited to a private screening of the director's cut of the film. Those attending the screening were all involved in the production end: producers, director, author, film editor, and so on.

I was the only actor there, perhaps because I had coached Barbara or because Herb Gardner wanted me there. The film we saw was a disaster. Usually at these screenings (or when watching dailies) the production people laugh their heads off at the slightest hint of an amusing moment. Here there was utter silence. The entire action took place in that one-room apartment, except for a brief scene on the staircase, and the audience came away with a feeling of claustrophobia. On top of that the camera was often not in the right place to capture a line or a reaction. Consequently, the laughs that we knew should be there were absent. Gene Saks, who had brought something special to his role on stage, was also missed.

Herb Gardner was not about to let this happen to his play. He went to the studio producers and made a deal. Herb would give up his screenwriting fee, and in return he would be allowed to reedit the film with his editor, Ralph Rosenblum. Herb would rewrite and take some scenes out to the street (including the end shot of Murray, in a suit and hat, briefcase in hand, trudging along with the rest of the crowd, returning to the job he had quit). Herb wanted to add the recorded marching music that was in the play but had been missing in the film, and he put Gene Saks back into the role of Chuckles.

The producers agreed, and the film disappeared for more than a year to be reworked. Herb told me Ralph Rosenblum's wife accused him of driving her husband mad, because Herb was insisting they go frame by frame and put back shots that were missing to recover the laughs.

More than a year after that dismal private screening, Barbara and I were both in a musical, *On a Clear Day You Can See Forever* (she in a starring role, I playing her boyfriend). We received an invitation to a midnight showing of the new version of *A Thousand Clowns*. There were the laughs, there was the music, there were the street scenes, and there was Gene Saks, as funny as ever. I left the theater amazed at the transformation. The film got excellent reviews, had a successful run, and it can still be seen on television some forty odd years later.

The cinematographer of *A Thousand Clowns*, Arthur Ornitz, must have known of my background working with Jerry Robbins because he called with an intriguing offer that I couldn't refuse. Arthur was about to work for the legendary Oscar-winning film director Joseph L. Mankiewicz (*All About Eve*, *Letter to Three Wives*), who was directing Rod Serling's adaptation of *A Christmas Carol*, scheduled to be broadcast on live television. It had an all-star cast, including Eva

Marie Saint, Sterling Hayden, Robert Shaw, and Peter Sellers. Would I be interested in being an assistant director on a project like that? He didn't have to ask twice.

I learned a lot watching Mankiewicz work. I liked the way he said to the actors "Whenever you're ready" instead of "Action!" and his notes were always sparing and precise. He quietly gave the cast a lot of freedom, and he was exactly the kind of director I liked to work with.

Peter Sellers had a bad heart, so I would do his lines when he was supposed to be off-camera resting. One day I was doing a spot-on impersonation of the comic master, and Robert Shaw, a superb British actor who would later star in *Jaws*, came up to me.

"What are you doing?" he asked.

"I'm filling in for Peter Sellers."

"You shouldn't be doing this. You should be in London, acting."

He went on to offer me his flat in London so I could go and establish myself with the acting community there, but I never took him up on it. We remained good friends until his early, untimely death.

My next play was Kirk Douglas's Broadway production of *One Flew Over the Cuckoo's Nest* in 1963. I say *Kirk Douglas's production* because he owned the stage and screen rights to Ken Kesey's novel, he hired the producer and director, and he starred in the show.

I was cast in the role of Dale Harding, a man who was running away from a marriage and any self-awareness by institutionalizing himself in a hospital full of mentally ill "cuckaboos."

Most of you know the story, but to summarize: there comes into the institutional nest a fairly sane man by the name of McMurphy who gathers these misfits together and gives them enough backbone to stand up to the big, bad Nurse Ratched. McMurphy, of course, was played by Kirk Douglas. In those days I didn't have the luxury of picking and choosing my roles; a job was a job and there was rent to be paid. If I'd had that luxury I would have turned down the role of Harding, but it was hard to say no to a Broadway play. It was one of the times I should have said no and didn't. Trouble started for me early in rehearsals.

As we began getting the play on its feet the director, Alex Segal, came to me and said my main scene, in which I explain why I was in this asylum in the first place, was to be cut. There I was again, fighting to preserve my role in the play.

"How can you cut something we haven't even blocked yet or seen how it would play?" I asked.

"Well, the play's a little long, and, well, it was Kirk's idea to cut it."

"But it explains why I'm in this darned place," I said.

"Let's go speak to Kirk about it," Alex said.

Big mistake. We went to Kirk's dressing room, where I made my plea about this speech being the crux of my part. Kirk, sitting at his makeup table, looked into the mirror in front of him and spoke to Alex in a very menacing tone: "Why did you bring him in here?"

That moment may have been the beginning of Alex's declining influence as director of the play.

"Billy, Billy, I don't want you to think that some Hollywood star is doing this play just for himself," Kirk said. "I think we're long, but I tell you what—let's stage it and see how it plays."

Once again, as in *A Thousand Clowns*, I had to fight for self-preservation in the role. The speech stayed in. I learned to stay alert when it came to dealing with Kirk, who had the habit of directing everyone around him and injecting pieces of business for himself that were not indicated in the play. For example, a few of us were seated around a table and Kirk suddenly pulled out a deck of cards and fanned them.

"Pick a card," he said, turning to me.

"Oh no, Kirk—you know Harding is in his own world," I said.

So Kirk turned the other way, toward Gerald S. O'Laughlin.

"Pick a card."

Gerald became the straight man and Kirk, what do you know, a magician! Apparently the play wasn't too long for this sort of addition. The director meanwhile sat in the back row of the orchestra reading the newspaper.

We tried out in New Haven, and most of the cast stayed at the Taft Hotel. I had the room next to Kirk's corner suite, and there was a door connecting both rooms. The door was so old it no longer hung properly, and you could see light coming from under it. One morning Kirk was doing vocal exercises, lots of "ohs" and "ahhs" and "moos" up and down the scale. It was very early, and after this had gone on for quite a while I went over to the door and yelled, "Gimme a stick and I'll kill it!"

I don't know what I expected to get—maybe a laugh or certainly an inquiry such as "Who said that?" But what I got was utter silence—and no more vocalizing in New Haven.

Bonnie made the trip up to see the show. Her critique of my performance was short and not so sweet.

"You look like you don't want to be up there on the stage," she said.

That about summed it up. It prompted me to put aside the distractions and get to work. The play opened at the Cort Theatre back in New York and ran for eighty-two performances.

On opening night Bonnie came into Sardi's looking for us and the opening night party (she was playing Off-Broadway in *Telemachus Clay* and couldn't attend the opening night performance). She found me seated at a table with some other cast members, including Gene Wilder and Jerry O'Laughlin.

"Where's the party?" she asked.

We pointed upstairs, where Kirk, Ethel Merman, and some big shots from Hollywood were celebrating with the VIPs; the cast wasn't invited.

The irony of this whole episode was that Kirk had always thought that he would make this play into a film starring himself. He tried for years to get it done; he even came backstage to my dressing room in *1776* wanting to know if I was still on board to play my old part. It wasn't until his son Michael took over the script that the award-winning film starring Jack Nicholson and directed by Milos Forman was made.

In my opinion the film is far superior, not only to the play but to Ken Kesey's book as well. One of the reasons is that Michael Douglas brought his great sense of humor to the project. I've known and liked Michael since he was a child, and his stepfather, Bill Darrid, who raised Michael with Kirk's first wife, Diana, actually became my best friend.

My story about Kirk Douglas may seem harsh. I've been accused of being an SOB, too, I'm sure, but I got to see the other side of him many years later when he made an important, selfless gesture at the beginning of my presidency at the Screen Actors Guild.

Broadway would not end for me on the sour note of *Cuckoo's Nest*. I had finally established a name for myself in New York, and there were many opportunities ahead.

10

On a Clear Day You Can See Paris

*O*n a Clear Day You Can See Forever was a musical written by Alan Jay Lerner with a score by Burton Lane. It was a show that was as overly long as its title, and that proved to be one of its problems. I was asked to have a meeting with Mr. Lerner, who informed me that he wanted me to take on the role of Warren Smith, the leading lady's boyfriend. Now Warren was a real schnook of a part, as dull as his name, and I told Mr. Lerner that I wasn't interested. But Alan Lerner was a man who was used to having his way.

"Suppose we write you a song?"

"I heard of an actor who went to Boston with three songs and came back with just a few lines," I said. *I don't know what possessed me to say that.*

"What if we guarantee that if the song is cut you can leave the show?" he asked.

My agent said she never heard of such an incredible offer and that I must do it. I realized that if the song was any good it would make a big impact on the role.

Once again my no was turned into a yes. It was becoming the story of my life.

Off I went to Boston for the show's out-of-town tryout. It turned out that the leading lady was to be my old friend and frequent colleague Barbara Harris, and the leading man was the film star Louis Jourdan, who had that French sex appeal. The song written for me was titled "Wait 'til You're Sixty-Five," and it was just one of many terrific songs that Alan Lerner and Burton Lane composed for this show (so terrific a score that Barbra Streisand later agreed to do the film for short salary).

At the first rehearsal with full orchestra in Boston I stood at the microphone to sing my number, the conductor gave the downbeat for this jazz waltz in three-quarter time with a blazing jazz riff from the trumpets, and I froze, mouth agape, overwhelmed by the music. The conductor stopped the orchestra and looked at me.

"That's your cue."

"Wow!"

"So take it from the top," he said, and this time I was smart enough to start singing.

As mentioned, the show had a number of problems, both inherent and created. Opening night in Boston the curtain went up at 7:30 and didn't come down until well after 11:00. Lerner insisted on seeing everything he had written, on the stage, before a live audience before he decided to cut anything. The story concerns a young lady (Barbara Harris) and a psychoanalyst (Louis Jourdan). Under hypnosis the woman reveals that she had lived a former life in the previous century. There was a whole cast of very good actors for the nineteenth-century section, and they had to be let go when the section was cut. How cruel this business can be.

Then Louis Jourdan was replaced, which to this day I believe was a mistake. They decided his singing voice was too light for the songs he had to sing, especially the powerful title song. In my opinion his voice may have been light, but he could have "talk sung" à la Rex Harrison and gotten through it, because what they were giving up was the chemistry that took place between this incredibly handsome Frenchman and this schlumpy young lady who melted at the very sight of him. Barbara Harris with her marvelous comic talent had the audience eating out of her hand, and the laughs were many. This chemistry was lost with Louis's replacement.

And then there was the unfortunate way the change took place. It was not announced to the cast, and we had *secret* afternoon rehearsals for breaking in John Cullum, a top-notch musical theater performer with a strong baritone that was much better than Louis's. (John and I would later work together again in *1776*, in which John played Rutledge and sang one of the best numbers, "Molasses to Rum.") We were told John was to go on only temporarily while Louis became familiar with "the revisions." Louis had to sit through those rehearsals in order to live up to the terms of his contract and be paid his salary for the run of the play. But how humiliating for him to have to do that and how cruel of them to handle it that way. It left a bad taste in my mouth and made me wary when Lerner came to me during rehearsals and said, "*Entre nous*, if anything is bothering Barbara, let me know."

It seemed he wanted me to be a go-between or, in other words, a spy. I would have none of that.

The musical opened to respectful reviews in New York and seemed to be settling in for a decent run. I don't recall how long into this run we were when I received a surprise call from my agent.

"You won't believe this, but I just received a cablegram sent from Shannon Airport in Ireland offering you a feature role in a film entitled *Two for the Road*, which is to star Audrey Hepburn and Albert Finney and is to be directed by Stanley Donen. It was signed by Mr. Donen!"

I didn't know Stanley Donen or anyone in the cast, nor did I know anyone at Twentieth Century Fox, the studio that was producing the picture. It would require me to spend a month in Paris (where I had never been) with a bunch of people I didn't know, with a script I had trouble following (different cars coming and going in different time frames).

To hell with Broadway and Warren Smith and "Wait 'til You're Sixty-Five"—Paris here I come!

It turned out that Stanley Donen had seen the film *A Thousand Clowns* on the plane when he was flying to Paris for the shoot and had decided on the spot to cast me and Barbara Harris. (Barbara would turn the film down to continue her lead role in the musical, saying, "I can't go—I'm a star.")

Stanley had one request of me before I left New York: he asked me to buy two loud, plaid madras sport coats (they couldn't find any in Paris.) Wearing those jackets in the film made me immediately identifiable as the "ugly American," and I think that's what they were going for.

After leaving *On a Clear Day*, though, I flew to Hollywood to do my first TV pilot—a half-hour comedy written and produced by

Buck Henry (someone else I had never met) and titled *Captain Nice*, a spoof on Superman. Buck Henry and Mel Brooks had created a huge hit at NBC—the hilarious *Get Smart*—and NBC had given Buck a chance to create his own project.

Then I left Hollywood and flew to Paris (on Air France, first class!) and arrived there late at night. On the flight over I began to have qualms about being met at the airport. I convinced myself that no one would be there to meet me, and, even if they were, no one would recognize me (nor me them.) So on landing I walked straight to the baggage claim, unknowingly passing a young lady who was waving the script of the film in the air and who, just as I suspected, didn't recognize me.

With suitcase in hand and knowing only one word of French, I pleaded with a cab driver, "Relais Bison, Relais Bison." That was the name of my hotel, which Buck Henry had told me was a favorite of Jackie Kennedy's, so what could go wrong? The driver had a lot to say and seemed unwilling to understand that I didn't speak French. I'm terrible at languages—I lived in Italy for two years while I was in the army and didn't learn one phrase of Italian. My favorite places to travel are England, Scotland, and Ireland, where the only language barrier is English.

Finally he said, "Ah! Relais Bisson!"—correcting my pronunciation in a nasty way. (It was obvious that he had understood me the whole time.)

"*Oui, oui*," I said, speaking the only French I knew.

Off we went to some little place on the Left Bank that looked to be in total darkness and in fact looked closed. However, the front door was open, and there, sitting behind a small reception desk, sat a very old man reading in a very dim light. The whole setting was spooky. After some difficulty the old man found my reservation and signed me in. Then he dragged my suitcase up some steps. I pointed to the elevator, but the man shook his head; evidently it closed down at night.

The next morning I called the number I was given for the film's office.

"Where were you?" someone asked.

"What do you mean?"

"We sent a girl. She was at the gate waving a script."

"Oh, I guess I didn't see her. Listen, you've got to get me out of here."

I moved to the Hotel Prince de Galles on the Right Bank, where there were working elevators and everyone understood English. I'm sure that Jackie Kennedy had a lovely time at the Relais Bisson—but then, she did speak French.

The following day I was driven out to the location where the company was shooting so that I could meet the director, as well as Ms. Hepburn and Mr. Finney.

My role—in fact the whole film—took place primarily on French country roads. And what roads they were—scenic and beautiful, often lined with cypress trees. There was a scene in a gorgeous country inn that had a small bridge over a pond with swans swimming by. I was beginning to feel better.

I had a costume fitting right there on location and then met the director Stanley Donen, who I subsequently learned was a highly thought of, successful director, particularly of musicals set to film. He gave me a brief rundown of how he thought my role should be realized. In short, I was *the ugly American.* I listened carefully and nodded in agreement and proceeded to do the part the way I thought it should go.

The qualities that Donen envisaged for my character were indeed apparent in the script, but it's a trap for actors to emphasize what is already there; what the actor must often do is find the character's human attributes other than what is written. Does he have humor? Does he have a warm and sympathetic side? Is he uptight and maybe even nervous or frightened (not that he would show it to his wife and child) while driving the roads of a foreign country and not speaking the language? My challenge was to come up with anything I could to humanize the man so as not to wind up with a caricature.

I met the rest of the cast and was driven back to my hotel with a call sheet informing me that in the morning I was to do my big scene—a quarrel and breakup with Mr. Finney's character that would lead to us going our separate ways (Finney's and Hepburn's characters had previously been hitching a ride with me and my screen family in our station wagon). Since most films are shot out of sequence, it often happens that you can wind up doing your most important scene on the first day, so I was up a good deal of the night learning the lines and pondering how it should be done. The next day, while they lit the scene using big reflectors to catch the sunlight, Finney and Hepburn were sitting in the back of the station wagon waiting to begin. I was pacing up and down under a tree, nervously going over my lines, when I heard a voice.

"Billy!" Finney was waving to me (actually with his index finger and smiling) to come over to the car. There he sat with Audrey Hepburn next to him, and he leaned out the car window and said in a stage whisper, "Not to worry, she gets all the close-ups." I heard her giggle.

And that was Albert Finney, sizing up my situation, breaking the ice with humor, and, more importantly, relaxing me. Everyone called him Albie. He was witty and great fun to be around. He was constantly teasing Audrey, calling her "tawdry Audrey" or "Audrey Sunburn."

When Bonnie arrived in Paris, having parked our children (babies, really) at her parents' home, she came out to location. When she was introduced to Finney as my wife, he took her hand in both of his, looked her in the eyes, and said, "Oh, I am so sorry."

Her knees didn't buckle the way they did when I first kissed her, but she might have been willing to run away with him at that moment. Albie was a real charmer. I have no insight into Albie and Audrey's relationship except to see what was obvious, that is, how well they worked together and what appeared to be an intimacy that must have developed over the months they spent together on this picture. Audrey was the consummate professional, always prepared and very focused. She must have sensed that *Two for the Road* would be one of her best film performances, particularly playing next to such a good actor. Even though it could be hot as hell out on those roads in August and most of the actors would need constant mopping up of perspiration before a take, not Audrey. She would sit under an umbrella by the roadside with not a drop of moisture on her.

At the wrap party she danced with just about every member of the crew. She danced until her feet actually bled. When she and Albie took Bonnie and me out to dinner at a terrible Italian restaurant in Paris (it was August, when all the best restaurants were closed, and Audrey had trouble with the rich French cuisine), she sat at the head of the table chatting away as if we were at Tour d'Argent, while Albie kept trying to feed Bonnie. In spite of the terrible food, it was one of the most entertaining dinners ever.

After we wrapped the film, I was told I'd have to stay and lip-sync everything I'd spoken in the film. Since most of the scenes took place outdoors, on the road, all the outdoor sounds had to be eliminated. I was very anxious to go home. Donen said he thought it would take me two days of recording. I got the knack of it pretty quickly and got through it all in one long recording session. Then I was homeward bound.

11

Buck and Mike

When I returned from Paris after wrapping *Two for the Road*, Alan Jay Lerner had an offer for me. It was delivered by the well-known choreographer Herb Ross, who I had worked with in *On a Clear Day You Can See Forever*. Lerner had written a new musical, and he wanted Herb to choreograph it and me to direct the book. But there was more. The musical was called *Coco* and was based on the life of Coco Chanel, and Katharine Hepburn had already agreed to play the title role.

As much as I respected Katharine Hepburn's abilities, it was difficult to see her, with that upper-class New England accent of hers, as a French icon. Without doubt, Katharine Hepburn was a great actress. Her classic films with Spencer Tracy are among my favorites, but Coco Chanel was tiny and I just couldn't see myself directing the statuesque Hepburn in that role. I didn't even know if she could sing. And would she attempt a French accent? Even if she did, what might that sound like? Her high, nasal, piercing voice was world famous. I would sooner have cast her as Jane in *Tarzan of the Apes*.

I turned down the offer. The show went on, had an eight-month run on Broadway, and made a profit.

Once again I had said no to a chance to direct. Even though I had been successful coaching actors and, in essence, "directing" for a long time, I came to realize that I didn't want to be a director and have the responsibility of coming up with what has been erroneously called a "vision." Directors supposedly have a "vision" of a play or film—they are supposed to have many or most of the production elements mapped out in their heads before they begin rehearsals. But my experience with directors has been the opposite, even for the great ones I've worked with. None of them really knew what they had at the very beginning, and if the project turned out to be something worthwhile, it was merely a matter of random luck. I didn't like that process and wanted no part of it.

Many times over the years I would be handed a project to direct and could see right away that it wasn't ready. However, I didn't have the "vision" to see how it could be fixed or turned into a winner. A good example is when George Furth approached me with a play about couples and their relationships, and he had the unique idea of one actress playing all the wives. It was charming and a lot of it was quite good, but it just wasn't strong enough. It was never made into a play, but when George got together with Stephen Sondheim on the project, it became the great musical *Company*, and that was most certainly a winner.

I did get one actual directing job in my life: an episode of *St. Elsewhere*. I had a wonderful time with my fellow cast members, and it was a well-written script about autism. The producers asked me to direct other episodes, but I turned them down because a TV director just has to set up shots as efficiently as possible and isn't given much room for creativity. Unlike the feature film industry, in which the director is "the creative," in TV it's the writers and producers, and a TV director simply doesn't have any creative control.

After withdrawing from *Coco* I received news that *Captain Nice* had been picked up by NBC for half a season (thirteen episodes). Buck Henry told me how he had chosen me for the lead role (even though we didn't know each other.) He said that he had a picture of an actor's face—someone he'd seen on stage or film but whose name he couldn't remember.

As Buck tells it, he was walking by a movie theater playing *A Thousand Clowns*, and there, on a poster outside the theater, was the picture of the actor he had in mind for the role. Thus was I cast. Throughout my career people have been trying to put a name to my face. I've heard innumerable people say, "I know you. What's your name again?"

Although I've had a long career, it irks me that some people in show business don't equate that longevity with success. For that crowd only stardom equals success. I walked out of the New York premiere party for *The Graduate* when the esteemed screenwriter William Goldman, who had written several excellent books about show business, said to me, "Oh, Billy, I want to write a book about you, George Grizzard, John McMartin, and other really good actors who've just never 'made it.'" I glared at him and said, "I don't want to be in that book," got up from the table, and was out the door, with Bonnie trailing behind. I walked right past Mike Nichols, who didn't see me and later told me that he didn't even know I'd come to the party.

A strange thing occurred just as we were beginning rehearsals of *Captain Nice*, the NBC spoof of Superman. CBS threatened NBC with a lawsuit, claiming that the idea for the show was stolen from them. The lawsuit went nowhere, but CBS went ahead and filmed another spoof of *Superman* and called it *Mr. Terrific*. The networks went ahead and committed mutual suicide by premiering their shows on the same night, with *Mr. Terrific* airing a half hour before *Captain Nice*. All I can say for our show is that it remained one of Grant Tinker's favorite shows (he was VP in charge of programming at NBC at the time). Neither show got past its original order.

But *Captain Nice* proved to be important for me inasmuch as it put me in contact with Buck Henry. After scripts were prepared by a number of writers, Buck was hired to write the screenplay that became the film *The Graduate*, directed by Mike Nichols.

As an ordinary actor, rather than a major star who gets involved at the very beginning of a film project, I seldom knew what sequence of events led to this or that job offer. In the case of *The Graduate* I still don't know.

It might have been Buck or it could even have been Mike Nichols who was behind the phone call offering me the role of a hotel clerk in Nichols's new film. By now you know me and you know that I turned it down. But then I received a phone call from Mike Nichols himself. He wanted to know why I turned down the role.

"It's a tiny part," I said.

"It's got two laughs," Mike said.

"I know that."

Then I went on a verbal rampage about how people in Hollywood did not know about the important parts I had played. It was a specious argument, since Mike Nichols was of New York, not Hollywood. Finally he interrupted my harangue.

"Bill, I didn't mean to insult you. I know what you can do. I've seen you in *The Zoo Story*, *A Thousand Clowns*, and *Look Back in Anger*." He may even have mentioned some other shows. But he managed to both shut me up and get my attention.

"How about playing one of the fathers?" he asked.

When I read the script, I'd never thought about those parts since there's barely a ten-year age difference between me and Dustin Hoffman, but now we were talking about a much bigger part.

"Take a look at it and come in and we'll talk about it," he said.

At the meeting the producer, Larry Turman, came right out and said, "Bill, I think you're too young to play Dustin's father."

Mike said, "You know that speech you had in *A Thousand Clowns*?" (I swear he then gave me the opening lines of that speech, the one I had had to fight for.) "I don't need that kind of self-awareness in this role," Mike said.

"Of course not," I said.

I left the meeting with the feeling that the producer's opinion would prevail. So when an offer came along to do a small (but funny) role in a film starring James Coburn called *The President's Analyst*, I took it. (That film became a cult favorite.) My scenes were shot in Washington DC, and when I returned to LA I had another call from Nichols.

"Why did you take another job? I want you in my film."

I thought he must have been joking, because I'd never gotten an offer, but there it was: I was to play Dustin Hoffman's father. There were to be three weeks of rehearsals before we started filming. We met on an empty soundstage at Universal Studios and had a table read of the script. Then we rehearsed individual scenes, but blocking the scenes remained loose since there were no sets or furniture or props, just white tape indicating different areas. I remember the tape that designated the area for the pool scene. Other than getting to know each other and maybe memorizing some lines, I'm not sure what was gained by these rehearsals. Nichols had lots of conversations with his cinematographer, Bob Surtees, who was always present, so perhaps Mike was working on their relationship and blocking camera shots.

During these rehearsals a very fine actor, Gene Hackman, who had been cast as Mr. Robinson, was let go, which might have made some of the cast apprehensive. (Dustin has been quoted as saying he thought he might be fired as well.) Nichols gathered the cast together and took full blame for having miscast Gene. (Gene's career recovered quite nicely.) After just two weeks of these rehearsals Nichols called them off, saying he was acting like we were an out-of-town tryout in New Haven.

"Go home, relax. I'll see you on location."

The shooting went along very pleasantly for me. Nichols didn't do much prompting and let me do my own thing. For me he always had the famous sense of humor he exhibited in the comedy duo of Nichols & May. I remember standing next to him at the pool of the Braddock house with the cinematographer while he considered how he was going to film the scene there. He became aware of me standing next to him.

"What?" he asked.

"I'm just curious as to how you're going to shoot this scene," I said.

Nichols turned to his assistant director.

"Why is he attacking me?" Nichols asked.

I also quickly learned not to sit next to Mike and Buck and try to join in on their humorous repartee; I was way out of my league.

I don't think anyone who worked on that picture had any notion of how important the film was to become. At one point early in rehearsals Mike gathered the cast together and said he wanted us to listen to some music by two young men he was considering as composers for the film ("one's tall and one's little"), and then he played for us the album *Sounds of Silence*. It was an eye-opening moment for me. I had thought the film was going to be a light comedy, directed by a Broadway director of light comedies (such as *Barefoot in the Park*), and featuring a Broadway star, Anne Bancroft. But this was serious music from two talented young men, expressing the feelings and concerns of a youthful generation. All eyes, it seemed to me, would turn to the star, the young Off-Broadway actor Dustin Hoffman; it was his film.

As a side note, and this is purely hearsay on my part, I had heard that Paramount wanted someone more prominent for the young male lead (such as Robert Redford, who was interested). They wanted Dustin to sign a three-picture deal, which he wisely refused. He made a hell of a lot more money on his next picture (*John Loves Mary*). I remember Dustin complaining to me that I was making more money than he was. In complete deadpan I offered to switch parts. He didn't take me up on it, and the role of Benjamin Braddock launched Dustin's film career.

The most important "vision" that Nichols brought to the film was the casting of Dustin—something he insisted on. At lunch with Nichols after we'd wrapped shooting, he was still wondering whether or not he would use the music of Simon & Garfunkel. His uncertainty backs up my idea that directing involves a lot of guesswork. Guesswork it is, but by talented people, making intuitive choices.

We had been living in Los Angeles for about a year so that I could film *Captain Nice* and *The Graduate*. It was during this busy year of 1967 that Sandy Dennis came to our home in Fryman Canyon (we were renting from Gordon MacRae) with the script of a two-character play called *Daphne in Cottage D*. She wanted me to do it with her on Broadway. Sandy was no longer just the girl I knew from *A Thousand Clowns*. Walter Kerr's love-letter review of her performance in *Any Wednesday* had made her a Broadway star. My reaction to the script was negative, as usual, but since that was how I greeted everything offered to me I was beginning to distrust my own knee-jerk reactions. Bonnie urged me to take on this leading-man role, something I'd never been offered before. So off we went to New York and into a nightmare.

I don't remember much about the rehearsal period except the realization that the director, an old friend of Sandy's and mine, Marty Fried, was not going to be much help in staging the play. The play also needed a third act, and we didn't have one that worked by the time we got to out-of-town tryouts in Providence and Boston. In

17. William Daniels in *Two for the Road* (production still), 1967. *Two for the Road* © 1967 by Twentieth Century Fox. All rights reserved.

18. William Daniels as John Adams in *1776* (Broadway production still), 1969. Photograph by Martha Swope. © The New York Public Library.

19. (*Above*) William Daniels as John Adams in the White House in front of the original painting of President John Adams, 1971. Source: *Washington Post*.

20. (*Opposite top*) William Daniels as John Quincy Adams in *The Adams Chronicles*, 1976. Photograph by Carl Samrock, used with permission of WNET.

21. (*Opposite bottom*) William Daniels as John Quincy Adams in *The Adams Chronicles*, 1976. Photograph by Carl Samrock, used with permission of WNET.

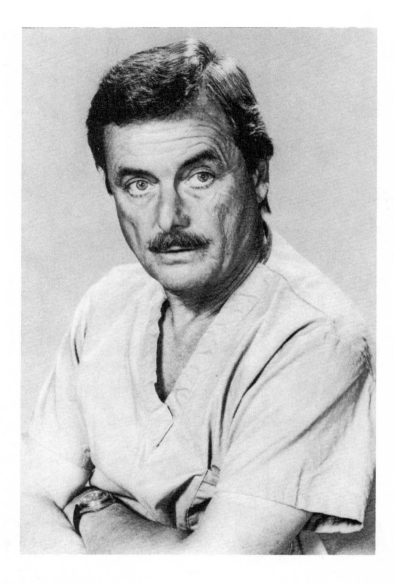

22. William Daniels as Dr. Craig
in *St. Elsewhere*, 1982.
Courtesy of author.

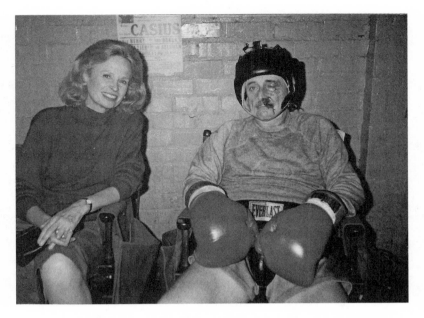

23. On the set with Bill and Bonnie, *St. Elsewhere*, 1980s. Courtesy of author.

24. William and Bonnie Bartlett Daniels at the Emmy Awards, 1986.
Source: Invision/Television Academy/AP Images.

25. William Daniels and David Hasselhoff (star of *Knight Rider*), 1982. Courtesy of author.

26. KITT, the car from *Knight Rider*, 1982. Courtesy of author.

27. William Daniels as Mr. Feeny with Ben Savage, 1993. © American Broadcasting Companies, Inc.

28. The cast of *Boy Meets World*, 1993. © American Broadcasting Companies, Inc.

29. The cast of *Boy Meets World* (with Danielle Fishel as Topanga), 1993. ©
American Broadcasting Companies, Inc.

30. Lin-Manuel Miranda and Bill backstage at *Hamilton*, 2016.
Courtesy of author.

addition, Sandy's performances there were met with silence and unease. You could sense that she and the role she was playing were turning off the audience, and that sent her into a panic.

There followed a seemingly endless series of rewrites that Sandy said were coming from a play doctor she had stashed away in our hotel. At each day's rehearsal we received new scenes or old scenes that had been rearranged in an attempt to make the play work. Our stage manager, who had been with us on *A Thousand Clowns*, took me aside one day and told me there was no play doctor. It was Sandy herself doing the rewrites. And to compound the problems, my role *did* seem to work. The reason my character was in a woman's cottage, drinking not half as much as she was until the wee hours of the morning, wasn't revealed until well into the play; the audience was curious to know more about him. When his tragic circumstances were revealed in a well-written monologue that stunned the audience, you could hear a pin drop. This reaction didn't sit well with Miss Dennis. She moved my monologue into the first act, then back into the second act, but nothing seemed to destroy it.

Each night became an emotional catharsis for her. All the bad habits she had exhibited in the crying scene in *A Thousand Clowns* that Jason had tried to rid her of came back in this play. This time, these proclivities appeared in not one but all of her scenes—the repetitions, the ad-libbing, the hemming and hawing, the snifflings, the crying, and so on. In her frustration and anger with the situation she decided one night to try and humiliate me in a scene in which my character is supposed to be leaving politely. In the scene I glanced at my watch and said I should go. She turned to the audience.

"Oh, he does that every night, looking at his watch. It isn't even a real watch," she said.

I stood there, stunned and then furious.

"Good night," I said. That wasn't in the script. I moved toward the cottage door to leave. I was going to leave the stage, leave the theater, and leave Boston, but she rushed over and threw herself up against the door, blocking my way.

"I'm sorry, I'm sorry, I won't do it again, I swear," she said in a stage whisper.

How we got back into the play I don't remember. But that was the end of our speaking to each other.

I asked to leave the play before we opened in New York and was threatened with a lawsuit. Opening night in New York, with all those revisions and rewrites in her head, she got lost in the middle of the second act and was completely *up*—she went and sat in the stage left window seat not a foot away from the stage manager, who was trying to find the place in the script where she had forgotten her lines, but she was ad-libbing so much that he didn't know where she was in the scene. I sat stage right, took a cigarette out of my silver cigarette case, lit it with my Dunhill lighter that the director insisted I have, and smoked while she carried on with what must have sounded like gibberish to the audience. The critics were sitting out there watching and so was my wife, but I didn't give a damn. I let Sandy hang. I knew where she had gone off-script, but before I walked to center stage to get her back on track I finished that entire cigarette. Seeing me approach, she jumped up from her seat and met me center stage. Rather than have me help her, she found the words she had been missing.

The play ran only long enough to qualify for filming, although no film emerged from this debacle. From my point of view the only good thing that came out of this experience was that it got me out of Hollywood and back to New York. I was there in the right place at the right time when the best role of my career came along.

12

1776

I had been cast in the film version of *On a Clear Day You Can See Forever*, starring Barbra Streisand, but I told the producer, Howard Koch, that I didn't want to reprise my role as Warren Smith. I thought the character was kind of a wimp, and I wanted to break free from that kind of part. Instead they offered me the role of a doctor, and I agreed.

I flew to Hollywood for the table read. The actor playing Warren Smith was not available, so I wound up reading his role at the table as well. The moment I got the first big laugh as Warren I knew I was in trouble. Barbra glanced in my direction and then buried her face in the script. The next thing I knew, Howard Koch was insisting that I play Warren. I said no.

Howard called again, telling me that Streisand had agreed to let me sing a duet with her in the film if I would play the part. Again I said no.

He called once again and offered more money—a lot more money. And so, reluctantly, I finally agreed.

After all that haggling you can imagine how awkward it was for me to call Howard and ask him to let me out of the film contract because I wanted to play an extraordinary role in an extraordinary Broadway musical.

I had first come in contact with the musical *1776* at a backers' audition in producer Norman Twain's living room. Norman held an option on it, and he presented the script and some songs from the score. I was unimpressed by the music, and when I read the script I found the dialogue stiff and unwieldy, as if it had come straight out of a history book. Indeed it might have, since the author was a New

Jersey history professor by the name of Sherman Edwards. As I said, I wasn't impressed with it, so I walked away and forgot about it.

Eventually the project wound up in the hands of Stuart Ostrow, who was wise enough to hand it over to writer Peter Stone. Peter did a powerful rewrite of this play, adding wit, speakable dialogue, and a dramatic thrust that culminated in a deeply moving finale. This improved script was sent to me with the request to audition for the role of John Adams. The new version was truly impressive, but was that enough to send me running to an audition? Of course not. I just didn't operate that way.

I ranted to Bonnie with words to this effect: "What is this? The founding fathers singing and dancing up on a stage? And this in the middle of the Vietnam War? How ridiculous!"

Bonnie looked at me and calmly said, "Bill, it's as if this part was written for you. However, that's a lot of singing, and I don't know if you can do it."

So off I went to the audition, going to the Forty-Sixth Street Theatre, where the show was scheduled to open. I found the stage door locked and no one in attendance. Maybe I was late. Perhaps I'd gotten the time wrong. There was nothing to do but go home. While I was waiting for the bus I said to myself, *Bill, you know, maybe you should call your agent—there may be some foul-up.* So I dragged my feet to the nearest public phone and called my agent, Harriet Kaplan.

"Where are you? They're waiting for you at the theater!" she said as soon as she picked up.

"I went to the theater. Nobody's there. The door is locked."

"What theater?" she yelled.

"The Forty-Sixth Street Theatre," I shouted back.

"They are waiting for you at the Ziegfeld Theatre! Take a cab! I'll pay for it!"

So I hung up and took a cab.

The stage door there wasn't locked, but the backstage was empty so I walked out onto the stage. There sat a piano and a pianist who, judging from the expression on his face, had been sitting there for quite a while. A voice from the back of the audience called out to me.

"Hi, Bill."

I couldn't see who was out there.

"Hello—I'm sorry for being late. I went to the wrong theater," I said.

The voice said, "That's all right, we just wanted to hear you sing something."

So I handed the sheet music of "Wait 'til You're Sixty-Five" to the pianist. I don't know if at this point I was befuddled or what, but here was a song I had sung umpteen times in *On a Clear Day*, and I got into the middle of it and went dry. I couldn't remember the words, so I stopped and said, "Huh, sorry . . . I haven't sung this for a while."

They laughed. It turned out that my audience was the producer Stuart Ostrow, the writers Peter Stone and Sherman Edwards, and the director Peter Hunt, none of whom I'd ever met. When I left the theater I thought, *You not only blew the lyric, you blew the job.* Little did I know they really did want me for the show, and so once again I had backed into a great role.

The next day I received a call from my agent saying I had been offered the role of John Adams. It would be by far the largest part I'd played on Broadway. I had nine songs, two of them solos—no wonder they wanted to hear me sing—and I didn't even get through the whole audition song. My usual reaction when I got a job was just that, it was a job; I'd try to do it to the best of my ability. But this was something more, or at least that's what it became.

We rehearsed at a large studio in Chelsea. The first day of rehearsal we immediately started to block the first act. There were no sit-down read-throughs of the play. The representatives of the thirteen colonies at the Second Continental Congress stood at their respective desks as John Adams stepped down front (in the actual performance he entered in front of the closed curtains and into a spotlight). And I began my opening lines: "I have come to the conclusion that one useless man is called a disgrace, that two are called a law firm, and that three or more become a congress. And by God, I have had this Congress!" I went on until the final line of the speech. "Good God, what in hell are they waiting for?"

At that the curtain flew up and a thunderous chorus of male voices burst into song:

Congress:
Sit down, John!
Sit down, John
For God's sake, John
Sit down!

The tremendous sound at the rehearsal nearly knocked me over. *My God, this is going to be good*, I thought. The song is a vocal battle between John Adams and Congress.

John Adams:
Vote yes!
Vote yes!
Vote for independency!

Congress:
Sit down, John!

And believe me, it never failed to get the audience's attention. As it turns out, the play was perfectly cast. There were no quiet conversations in *1776*, only sharp confrontations. These were men torn between their desire for independence and their fear of being tried for treason.

Howard Da Silva bore a strong resemblance onstage to Benjamin Franklin. Ken Howard was as tall as Jefferson. Thank God the general public for the most part had no idea of what Adams looked like, because I bore no resemblance to the man, except perhaps for his energy—and his commitment. I became committed to this role in a way I have never done with any other. And I played Adams for almost a thousand performances, which included a lengthy out-of-town tryout and more than two years on Broadway. The great historian David McCullough sent me a copy of his book *John Adams* and inscribed it with this: "For Bill Daniels, who knows the man and the story as few do."

Howard Da Silva, with whom I had worked in *Dear Me, the Sky Is*

Falling, was an excellent choice for Franklin. He was a strong actor with a strong voice, and he had already had a long career in theater and film (he was the original Jud in *Oklahoma!*). We became good friends and respected each other. Da Silva had great stage presence, but he wasn't above trying to steal a scene when he could. In early rehearsals I came offstage after having played a scene with him and muttered to an actor standing next to me, "Boy, I'm tired."

The actor, Scott Jarvis, who played Washington's young messenger, said, "He's leaning on you."

"What?"

"He's leaning on you, like a fighter who leans on you and wears you down."

Howard Da Silva was a hulk of a man, very tall and more than two hundred pounds. In the scene he would throw his arm around me, look down on me, say his lines, and lean his full weight on me; no wonder I was getting tired. In that stage image he created I must surely have disappeared.

The next time the scene came up at rehearsal and Da Silva approached, I put my cane to his chest and said, "We're politicians, Howard. We need space to be heard." And that put an end to his leaning on me.

Da Silva was the definition of a stage trouper who lived by the rule "the show must go on." On opening night at the Forty-Sixth Street Theatre in New York, Howard finished his performance while an ambulance waited outside to take him to the hospital to deal with a recurring heart problem. He was out for several weeks and unfortunately missed the recording of the cast album.

Playing my character's wife, Abigail Adams, was the talented singer and actress Virginia Vestoff, who, sadly, died at an early age from cancer. (It was during the run of *St. Elsewhere* that someone told me she was sick. I sent flowers with a card saying, "Yours, John"— like the lyrics from our duet—but the bouquet didn't arrive in time because the delivery drivers were on strike.)

The rehearsals for *1776* went smoothly enough. The young director's staging was fluid and easy for the actors, many of whom were primarily singers. This was Peter Hunt's first time directing a Broadway show, and he handled it extremely well. He was full of energy and enthusiasm and quick to laugh at the wit that Peter Stone had injected into the dialogue, and the laughter was genuine.

It was around the second week of rehearsals that the director asked me to join him for a drink.

We sat in a booth at a bar and Peter said, "You have my permission to kick my ass around the block."

I got the message: I hadn't been his first choice for the part, and I suppose he didn't want me to hear it from someone else.

After rehearsing for three or four weeks, off we went for a tryout in New Haven. We continued rehearsing, now with full orchestra, and I soon realized how vocally demanding this role would be. Eight performances a week, and it wasn't just the singing—Adams was a lawyer and an orator, and much of what he said was recorded in historical documents. When he took the floor in Congress, what he had to say wasn't muttered or conversational; it was declarative and persuasive and challenging to his fellow representatives. The effort and vocal strain were exhausting.

I worked on a regular basis with the vocal coach Keith Davis, who was famous for working with actors who sang in Broadway musicals. He literally saved their voices with proper breathing, support, and placement.

During the ensuing long run of *1776* I would, after eight performances a week, have no voice left by Sunday. Monday, Keith, with a series of exercises, would get my vocal folds in contact again in time for Monday night's performance. It became my routine, twice a week, Monday and Thursday (after Wednesday's two performances).

We opened in Boston to mixed reviews, but changes were made in rehearsals during the out-of-town tryout. The original choreographer was let go for, I believe, overchoreographing the show, and Onna White was brought in. She immediately simplified all the movements and staged just one actual dance. It was an elegant and smug minuet, performed by the right-wing members of the assemblage (mostly southerners), called "Cool, Cool, Considerate Men." Many people who have seen the show and even those of us involved in it inaccurately remember the song as "Cool,

Cool, *Conservative* Men"—because that's what we "heard" in the lyrics, but that lyric was never there. Stuart Ostrow did not want to offend anyone.

"To the right, always to the right," so the lyrics go.

Another change was a scene that proved to be extraneous and was omitted. This scene was right out of the history books: while traveling in a storm Franklin and Adams were forced to spend a night in a whorehouse. It was an amusing scene but interrupted the flow of the play. A song titled "The Egg" replaced that scene during the out-of-town tryout. As I've mentioned before, there are choices, right or wrong, that can make or break a production; these were the right ones.

In New Haven we were well received, even though we were faced with a big snowstorm and the audiences were small. The reviews were forgettable. It wasn't until we opened in Washington DC that we realized we had a hit show on our hands. The reviews were ecstatic and the houses sold out.

My fears that it might be bad timing to mount a patriotic play in the midst of the Vietnam War were laid to rest.

Never ones to miss a little flag waving, Congress came out in full force to see the show. I was introduced to Senator Edward Kennedy and his children before one of the matinees. It was there that Howard Da Silva and Ken Howard and I learned the new song "The Egg," and it was there that I got a new lyric in the afternoon to be inserted in the song. That night, I messed it up. God, I felt humiliated! The director and producer laughed about it later, but I suppose I was still back in that car going over the Queensboro Bridge with my mother saying, "What was so hard about that?"

Bonnie and I recently had the occasion to visit the theater library at Lincoln Center, where a friend of hers (Rod Bladel) has worked for years, and he showed us some of the reviews *1776* got for the opening in New York. I was surprised and amazed at the glowing personal reviews that I got, particularly the one by Walter Kerr, whom I greatly respected as a critic, as well as Brooks Atkinson's. Again, I only remember the bad reviews (like the one that lambasted me even though it was Veronica Lake who'd forgotten her lines).

So there we were, a Broadway hit that no one in New York expected. And we were in for a long run.

We opened rather late in the theater season (the latter part of March 1969), certainly a last-minute entry to be in contention for the Tony Awards. Nevertheless, *1776* won a Tony for Best Musical in 1969.

I was nominated in the Best Supporting or Featured Actor in a Musical category. My question was: whom was I supporting? I informed the League of New York Theatres, which ran the awards, that they should remove my name from nomination in that category. My reasons were obvious: I had the leading role in the play and got star billing (albeit below the title). I would have an unfair advantage against the true supporting actors in this category (in fact, Ron Holgate, in the marvelous supporting role of Richard Henry Lee in *1776*, won in that category). I received a phone call from Alexander Cohen, who was producing the Tony Awards show that year, wanting to know why I was withdrawing my name. When I explained, he complained that I was leaving him one short in the supporting role category.

"The leading role category is full and requires you to have star billing above the title," he said.

This "above the title" rule was changed the next year. I ended the conversation with my wish to have my name removed from the nominations, and I assured him I wouldn't be attending the ceremony. Bonnie was devastated and watched it on TV. I didn't.

How do I explain what it was like playing the role of John Adams almost a thousand times? Going to the theater six days a week and giving eight performances in a very demanding role?

I was forty-two years old when we opened in 1969, and I must have had the stamina of a younger man because I missed only two performances in those two years plus—once because I had one too many drinks with a visitor in my dressing room after a matinee and once after performing at the White House.

The first few months went by easily, but the work began to weigh on me. I've always been a nervous performer. About what? I don't know. About getting up to speed, about not screwing up, but mostly about *getting it right*.

There came a time that just knowing I had to go in there again caused my stomach muscles to knot up at about four o'clock in the afternoon. I found myself getting to the theater an hour earlier than was necessary just to pull myself together and start to focus on what I had to do onstage.

There were perks, of course. The star's dressing room, the personal dresser who attended your every need (hot lemon tea waiting for you at intermission), the respect you received from your coworkers onstage and off, and finally the applause (Bonnie insists that I never learned how to take a proper bow—it was always short and perfunctory, as if I couldn't wait to get on the bus to go home.) The applause simply meant *I got it right*, that the audience wasn't disappointed. It didn't fill me with a glow from all this "love" pouring forth toward me and all that nonsense. It was just the end of another performance.

It must have been during our first year's run that our producer received a request from the White House for a command performance of *1776*. It was the Nixon White House, and the request came with the caveat that we should remove the musical number "Cool, Cool, Considerate Men." In the song, the southern conservatives, who are against a declaration of independence (particularly if it contained an emancipation proclamation abolishing slavery) dance in step with a smug, self-righteous air of superiority that eerily resembles today's conservatives in Congress. Stuart Ostrow, our producer, refused to make that musical cut and declined the White House's invitation.

These requests evidently went on for some time, but it wasn't until the second year of our run when the message came that we would be allowed to do the entire show. Stuart called me to ask if I would go down to Washington to give a performance on Sunday evening, after having given eight performances during the week. Stuart, like me, was a liberal Democrat, and he listened quietly while I ranted about how much I loathed the Nixon administration. Stuart pointed out that regardless of who was presiding at the White House, it was still an honor to be asked and that it was good publicity for the show. Then he hit me with the clincher—the cast, for that single performance, would receive a week's salary. (Not only did I not receive a week's salary for the performance, but by not having Sunday off to rest my voice I missed Monday's show and my salary was docked for one performance.)

After Saturday night's performance in New York we all took the train down to Washington. This classy administration hadn't bothered to invite the wives of the cast, and Bonnie made such a fuss about it that Mrs. Nixon personally invited all the wives. Bonnie and I were put up in a lovely room at the Hay-Adams Hotel with a magnificent view of the White House all lit up at night—very impressive.

We rehearsed all Sunday afternoon with the Marine Band, which didn't seem to have a "pianissimo" in its repertoire. Perhaps that was because the band was stationed in the hallway outside the East Room and thus had to play loudly enough for us to hear from inside. We performed on a portable stage designed by Jo Mielziner (who had also designed our sets). It was a small stage for such a large cast, but we all knew the play well enough not to bump into each other. Even though we couldn't see the band or the conductor, the evening's performance went as well as could be expected under the circumstances. The round of applause from the several hundred in the audience prompted the president to come up onstage to say a few words. He inadvertently got a laugh in his opening remarks, which led to his going on a little too long.

There was some irony for Howard Da Silva to be standing next to the president, since Howard's Hollywood career had been one of those destroyed by the blacklist and the House Un-American Activities Committee (HUAC), a committee in which Nixon had actively participated.

After the performance everyone was herded into the beautiful main room with its famous paintings hanging over fireplaces. It looked like an old southern mansion, complete with black servants quietly serving drinks. This gathering was followed by a reception line to meet the president and First Lady. As I reluctantly stood on the line to meet them, a White House butler took my much-needed drink out of my hand so that I would be unencumbered for the meeting.

"He had an unhappy presidency, didn't he?" the president said, referring to John Adams.

"Yes, sir. I believe he did," I replied.

"Did you see his quotation over the fireplace in the State Dining Room?" Mr. Nixon asked.

That gave me pause because the cast had had lunch in the State Dining Room, and I had been seated next to the fireplace with the engraved quote of Adams above it: "May none but Honest and Wise Men ever rule under this roof."

Some of the cast teased me about it during lunch, knowing how I felt about the current president and the scurrilous details that were unfolding about him in the press regarding Watergate.

"Yes, sir, and I read that Abigail didn't care for Washington DC," I mumbled to Nixon.

With that I retired to the sidelines while Bonnie was greeted by the president. I stood next to three women of the press corps, one of whom was Helen Thomas (forced to retire in 2010 after making some antisemitic remarks in public). I waited for Bonnie, who seemed to be having a jolly good time chatting with the president. It went on for a little longer than most of the greetings.

Helen Thomas turned to me and asked, "What is your wife talking to the president about?"

"I believe he's discussing his upcoming divorce." I was playing for a laugh, but what I got was a couple of gasps and an "Oh my God."

"I was only joking," I hastened to add.

Bonnie was happily mentioning all the big fundraisers and supporters Nixon had in Moline, where she'd grown up, with those supporters including her brother. But then Bonnie always knew how to break the ice with strangers, even a president.

Doing eight performances a week can be stressful, and I must have mentioned it to our orchestra conductor, Peter Howard. He offered some advice.

"You know what? After the show, when you go home, you could do something relaxing, something that would be a change of pace. Why not learn to play the guitar? It's quiet. You wouldn't wake the family."

Peter put me in touch with a guy in the orchestra, an Italian who played the guitar. He found me a classical guitar made in Barcelona and started me out in the classical style. I went to his little studio in Chelsea once a week for almost a year and enjoyed every moment of it. I always looked forward to going home to the guitar, and it really helped me get through those eight performances a week.

Peter also found me a Yamaha piano with a wonderful sound for the incredibly low price of three hundred dollars.

Both of my sons, Michael and Robert, learned to play on that instrument. It traveled with us from New York to Los Angeles, and it now resides in Michael's house, where he uses it to prepare for his singing engagements. He sings with LA Opera, as well as for any number of churches and synagogues in the LA area. You might say we've gotten our money's worth out of that little spinet.

It was in the second year of my playing John Adams that a welcome diversion came to me in the person of actor Austin Pendleton, my old pal from the days of *Oh Dad*. Austin was writing a musical (with Gretchen Cryer) in which the main character was to be Junius Brutus Booth, the famous nineteenth-century Shakespearean actor and father of the even more famous American actor Edwin Booth and the infamous John Wilkes Booth. The plot was to follow Junius as he toured the country on horseback, stopping wherever a stage existed to play all the great Shakespearean roles—*Richard II* and *III*, *Macbeth*, and most famously *King Lear*—often with his young son Edwin along to help keep him sober enough to manage his next performance. I thought Austin's concept of imagining the trials and tribulations of this man and his son had great theatrical possibilities, and when he asked me to help structure his play and perhaps direct it as well, I readily agreed. Much of the play was written, but Austin was looking for a second act and an ending. I remember us doing some research in the second-floor library of The Players—a club that Edwin Booth founded—looking for references to Junius that might provide us with facts of his life that could translate into a dramatic narrative. Since I was still doing eight *1776* performances a week I had limited time for this project, but I enjoyed working with Austin tremendously. The play was to be called *Booth Is Back in Town*.

I had envisioned it as being done Off-Broadway, where it might have a better chance of success. I felt that the critics wore two different hats when reviewing Broadway and Off-Broadway productions, and our chances would be better downtown. But none of this happened in the end because things began to unravel when the young producer brought Jason Robards Jr. into the project. I was too busy with my own acting job and was not involved in the producing end. With no official capacity beyond the possibility of directing, I didn't feel entitled to object to an idea that everyone found so exciting— Jason Robards, a Broadway star, playing the elder Booth. And of course Jason was interested in playing the part of a great actor.

And then someone asked, "How about doing it on Broadway?" *Booth Is Back in Town* at the Booth Theatre! Starring Jason Robards Jr.! Of course no one on the project knew Jason as well as I did. I began to have doubts about the project. I didn't believe the play (as yet incomplete) was strong enough for Broadway, and I didn't relish the thought that my directorial debut would include managing Jason Robards, with his history of drinking.

This is what settled it for me: a backers' dinner, which would include several CBS executives, had been arranged at Sardi's restaurant. There were at least eight or ten investors in attendance along with the producer, the author, and myself. But the main attraction was Jason. He was flying in from Washington, where he was performing in a play with Maureen Stapleton. It was Sunday, his day off, and when Jason arrived at Sardi's he was already drunk. As the evening progressed he continued to drink, sitting in the middle of all those admirers, all laughing at his somewhat fumbled jokes. The laughter encouraged him to climb onto the dinner table to recite some poetry.

At that point it became necessary to get him off the table and out of the restaurant. Since I was the only one there who actually knew Jason, it fell to me to instruct our young producer that he must guide Jason out, get him into his waiting limousine, and stay with him until he was seated in the plane, because otherwise the crew would not let him on board.

That was the end of *Booth Is Back in Town* for me and for Broadway, though it lived to be produced in other, smaller venues. Jason called me a few days after this episode. I still don't know if he remembered what had happened that night, but after a few brief words of greeting I told him I had withdrawn from the show and that was that. Once again I had gone to the brink of directing and pulled away.

Jason's drinking may have put an end to *Booth* on Broadway, but you know what they say about letting he who is without sin cast the first stone. Over the years I had my own problem with alcohol. I didn't binge or disappear for days, and drinking rarely affected my work, but that hardly excuses me for drinking too much and too often.

Once I was out pub-hopping with several of the guys in the cast of *1776* while we were filming in Hollywood. I didn't think I had had that much to drink when we made our second stop at a bar near Universal Studios. It was one of those places that had the bar extending all along the back wall, with a small section at the end, and in that section sat a young lady with very blond hair that fell over her shoulders and veiled her face as she leaned over a chessboard. The guys from the cast sat down at the long part of the bar, but I walked toward the blond.

"Did you follow the Fischer-Spassky chess match in Reykjavik?" I asked her.

She nodded, so I sat down next to her.

I noticed the guys poking each other and grinning, but I figured, *So what? I was just having a conversation.* I looked at the chessboard and said, "It looks to me that white has the better position."

She nodded again. Sniggers erupted from the guys, but I also saw the bartender looking our way and grinning; that made me lean over the bar to get a look at her face and see if she had noticed all this attention. What I saw was that I was talking to a mannequin, a dummy. I approached the bartender, and he showed me the controls he had under the bar that made her nod.

"Very funny. I'll have a Stoli on the rocks," I said as I sat down with my friends. They were having trouble containing their laughter, but who could blame them?

13

Hooray for Hollywood

Opening night of the film *1776* was at the Ziegfeld Theatre in 1972. I remember me running out of the place and Stuart Ostrow running after me, yelling, "Bill, wait up." I didn't. I fled. I was disappointed with what we'd done. I felt that the stage play had a certain style that was missing from the film.

In the theater version the audience sits before a curtain, the lights go down, the curtain goes up, and there they see Jo Mielziner's version of Independence Hall with actors playing well-known founding fathers; then we ask the audience to suspend their disbelief and accept the artifice of the play. They are able to do this if the production adheres to some logic and the "make-believe" makes some sense, which enables the audience to accept the play's reality. But a film is a realistic medium, and I felt that at the opening of the film we had to, in some way, tie it into the artifice of the play so the audience would accept the founding fathers' singing and dancing in front of them. I had in mind something like what Laurence Olivier had devised for *Henry V*, in which a camera on high slowly descended onto the image of the Globe Theatre and then into it and finally into the film, thereby telling the audience that this is a play that is now becoming a film. I pictured Adams entering from behind a stage curtain and saying his opening speech in front of the curtain, ending with the opening of the curtain. We then find ourselves in Independence Hall and then in the film. I suggested this to the author Peter Stone. I thought it would be a simple retake of me in front of the curtain, but the film was already in the can and that was that.

I had spent thirteen weeks in Los Angeles filming *1776*, and I think it was during that time that the thought of living in California started brewing in me. I had never cared for Manhattan; why would I after all those early years of being dragged into the city to perform? At the end of my two and a half years with *1776* on Broadway, I never wanted to see a dressing room again. I wanted to run away from it all. And boy did I run. I ran from Bob Fosse's offer of the lead in *Chicago* and from another offer to do a British play (with Sandy Dennis and Geraldine Page). If we moved to California, though, I'd have to deal with my parents and sisters, all of whom had migrated to LA years before. But I wasn't too worried about that. For years I had kept them at arm's length—even my sisters, due to their bad marriages—and they had long ago accepted that. We would become much closer, as it turned out, once they all developed a relationship with my children.

I'm sure Bonnie thought I was making a mistake when I called her to say I'd found a house I wanted to buy in Studio City in the San Fernando Valley. Previously, while I was doing some television shows in LA, my father had driven me around the Studio City area looking at real estate. And we had spent a year living in the Gordon MacRae house in Fryman Canyon while I was doing *Captain Nice*, *The Graduate*, and other work in Hollywood. Bonnie loved Studio City, but she didn't want to leave New York.

Bonnie told me point blank that she wasn't moving to Los Angeles. She didn't want to take the children out of school or leave our apartment and all our friends. Adding to that, our marriage was on the rocks at that point, mostly because of my bad behavior from having one too many "on the rocks."

A word or two—perhaps a page or two—about drinking. I was fifteen and working as an assistant stage manager in *Life with Father* when, between matinee and evening performances, I walked from the theater across the street to a bar where the stagehands hung out, sat down at a small table, and ordered a manhattan. I didn't even know what was in it, but somewhere I'd heard it ordered before. I was a rather youngish-looking fifteen-year-old, and I wasn't certain I'd be served a drink, but lo and behold a waitress arrived with a rust-colored liquid that had a cherry lying at the bottom of the glass. I remember the first sip burned like hell, but the rest of it went down all right, right into my empty stomach. What didn't go right was when I stood up. I was woozy, and that frightened me because I knew I had the evening performance to get through. I was stage managing on that show, and thank God I didn't have to be *on* the stage.

That was the first and last drink I had for a very long time. I didn't drink during my two and a half remaining years with *Life with Father*, not once at Northwestern, nor during my two years in the army (even though there was that fully stocked bar in the backyard of the radio station in Livorno), and certainly not when I was down and out looking for an acting job in the 1950s.

My next drink was not one but a couple of drinks—again between the matinee and evening performance—this time while I was doing *The Zoo Story*. There are many legendary stories of the great British actors getting bombed during intermission (or "the interval" as they call it), but I guess they have the constitution to do that. For me, I remember being a little slow to respond when my lines came up and being very careful with my pronunciation. It scared the hell out of me, and it didn't happen again until many years later—again while socializing between matinee and evening performance. This time I was entertaining guests in my star's dressing room during the run of *1776*. I wasn't exactly drunk—a little tipsy maybe—but I wasn't up to the demands of performing the role of John Adams that evening. I simply told a stunned stage manager that I wasn't feeling well and left the theater.

Was I drunk? I remember I went home and persuaded Bonnie to go to the movies at a theater downtown, not far from where I was supposed to be working. I felt like I was playing hooky—and it felt great.

Steady drinking started with my gradual success in New York theater—the two things seemed to go hand in hand. What's the first thing just about every cast member says after an evening performance? "Where are we going to drink tonight?" Over the years—and to this day—there have been bars near Times Square where all or most of the Broadway actors go to drink until the wee hours. Ironically, one that was around for a long time was called Barrymore's. This boozing isn't true of every actor, of course. Bonnie never had more than one glass of wine before calling it a night.

Bonnie insists that I had become an alcoholic because I drank every night and that doing so had caused my personality to change, from angry and hostile to *really* angry and hostile. There are degrees of alcoholism, and I was neither a binge drinker who disappeared for days, like Jason Robards, nor a falling-down drunk (except once at the SAG Awards, where I was in agony—and yes, when I got to my house I fell down in the foyer, drunk and happy to be home.) I've never chosen to go into treatment or anything like that, and I still enjoy a good glass of wine or two.

There's no doubt that my New York drinking made me hard to live with and put a huge strain on my marriage. I don't think Bonnie wanted to go to LA or anywhere else with me for that matter. But I asked her to just come for the summer and see how she liked it. We'd keep the apartment we owned in New York.

So the move was made.

I introduced Bonnie to my Hollywood agents, and after that she never stopped working in television. She got a recurring role in the hugely successful *Little House on the Prairie*, and that settled the whole question of where we would live. We moved into a lovely "little house" of our own in the flats of Studio City. It sat on a corner lot and had three bedrooms and even a pool. We found the boys a lovely school (the Mirman School) on Mulholland Drive atop the mountain, and we settled in. There's a cliché that Hollywood ruins marriages. I can honestly say that it saved mine. We were both working—in the same town—and every night we were able to go to bed together in the same house.

The only fly in the ointment was that there was very little acting work for me in film or television. I got a lot of "How long are you out here for?" or "When are you going back to New York?" It seemed everyone thought of me as a New York actor.

But there was more to it than that. As far as TV goes, Hollywood is a company town. And for the actor that means "Have you worked recently in film or TV?" They say "recently" because the productive lives of producers, directors, and writers can be very brief. There is a tremendous turnover in all those jobs. Couple that with the fact that I had signed up with only mid-level agents and that my last

TV series, *Captain Nice*, was a decade old. As for films, *The Graduate* was already five years in the past; it was clear that I was in for a long haul before I was going to make a decent living at acting. And so it was that in the 1970s I took some pretty pathetic parts to pay the mortgage.

I remember I took the part of a clown in *Battlestar Galactica*. My character, Norman, didn't have a last name, he didn't have much to say, and I thought with the clown makeup, the orange wig, and the bulbous nose I could quietly do the part without anybody noticing. Well, in the script Norman is in a car accident and as he's being wheeled into the emergency room on a gurney, the director said, "Bill, at this point, why don't you take off the wig and the nose so we can see who you are."

My head shot up.

"My God, no! This guy's been in a car accident! He's practically comatose," I said.

"Oh, okay," the director said.

I lay back down and closed my eyes.

I did two episodes of *The Rockford Files*, which starred James Garner. It was on the second one that I was rehearsing a fight scene and was thrown around by an overzealous young actor who, instead of "marking" the fight moves, went at it full throttle in rehearsal and hurled me against the arms of a metal chair. I was sent to St. Joseph's Hospital, not far from Universal Studios, where X-rays were taken, and then I returned to work.

I was lying down in my dressing room when Jim Garner came in and asked how I was doing.

"Okay," I said. "But it hurts when I breathe."

"What did they say at the hospital?" he asked.

"They said I was all clear to go."

Jim was very protective of me and mumbled something about not trusting the studio or the hospital. He had the X-rays sent up to his Beverly Hills doctor and set up an appointment for me.

The doctor hung up the X-rays and took out a black marker.

"This is a broken rib and this is a broken rib, and so is this," he said, drawing on the X-rays.

So I was out of the show and, come to think of it, out of the pay-check for it. I didn't get a nickel from the show or from Universal Studios for my work.

But I've always appreciated Jim's concern. Jim, by the way, never trusted the studio about anything related to the show and later won millions of dollars in a lawsuit, collecting profits from the show that the studio had tried to hide.

Not all the parts I took were terrible. I was cast in a television play called *The Lie*. It was a small part, just one scene, but the play was written by Ingmar Bergman and anything he wrote was at least interesting. And so was this scene between an institutionalized brother, played by me, and his visiting sister, played by Shirley Knight. She came into his hospital room and found her brother lying in bed and all decked out in jewelry—earrings, bracelets, and a necklace. The conversation was cursory, with long pauses, but as written it created a great tension as she avoided mentioning the jewelry and he took pleasure in her discomfort. I asked the director, Alex Segal, why the jewelry? When he asked Bergman about that, the answer he got was, "Oh, he just felt like wearing it that day," which I took to mean, "Let the actors figure it out!" And we did. Whenever there was a silence in our talk, I played with the jewelry as might a woman who was on the make. It forced the sister to look away at those moments, and the tension in the scene increased. We never got any feedback from Bergman, so I don't know if he approved of our interpretation, or if in fact he ever saw this American production of his play.

Another exceptional role was playing Elizabeth Montgomery's lawyer in the TV film *A Case of Rape*, which was way ahead of its time and considered quite controversial at the time.

In the 1970s scripted programs on cable television didn't exist, so all the one-hour dramas were squeezed into the three networks: NBC, ABC, and CBS. In addition to *The Rockford Files* I did shows like *McMillan & Wife*, *Quincy M.E.*, *McCloud*, and so forth. Even if you managed to do three or four spots a year, you weren't making a living. Fortunately, Bonnie was working fairly steadily during that time, so we managed.

Most of the shows I did were forgettable pilots that never went to series—shows with laughable names like *Rooster*, *Big Bob Johnson*, *Fabulous Dr. Fable*, and *Life in Desire*. No one knows if a pilot is going to be picked up, but to protect themselves the producers usually offer a pretty good salary to the series regulars to ensure that they will agree to be put under contract if the series goes. The salary I received for one of these pilots was often enough to get us through the entire year of expenses, including private school tuition for our boys.

A couple of shows actually did make it to the air but lasted for only thirteen episodes, the minimum order that networks made in those days. One was based on the film *Freebie and the Bean* and the other was *The Nancy Walker Show*. Both shows actually had some potential—the *Freebie* pilot had some good writing and good acting (from Hector Elizondo, for example), but the network destroyed it when it got to series, insisting that every episode be nothing more than one big car chase. Nancy Walker was a victim of Nancy Walker. She was a wonderful comedienne, but as executive producer she insisted on playing it "straight," as a romantic leading lady. I'm not sure what the king of TV comedy, Norman Lear, thought about that. He was also one of the show's creators.

Most of the pilots I did in the 1970s were destined for failure—you could just tell from the script. It took about a decade of such work until I finally read some good TV scripts—and they happened to be the first five episodes of *St. Elsewhere*.

During my years in the TV desert I managed to make another outstanding film. Alan Pakula cast me in a small but interesting part in *The Parallax View*. It was 1974 and conspiracy was still in the air (thanks to Vietnam and the Nixon years), and that was the implied subject of the picture. It was never explicit, but hauntingly present. My part, Austin Tucker, was as chief of staff for a senator who is assassinated in the meeting hall atop the Space Needle in Seattle. Tucker, who was at the senator's side when the killing takes place, flees the scene, leaving everyone to wonder whether he fled in fear or if he was somehow involved in the crime.

Warren Beatty was the star of the film, and I had several scenes with him. In one scene Warren and I are sitting in the cabin of a small motor launch, and in the back, standing at the steering wheel of the boat, was this rather rugged, good-looking actor. There was no dialogue in the scene (later the boat explodes with me but not Warren in it). So there we were, Warren and I, sitting side by side, saying nothing. I got an idea. *Why not make my character, Austin Tucker, gay? There's a handsome guy at the wheel . . . I could just stare at him.* The actor at the wheel seemed to pick up on it and stared back and smiled. Our smiles were small, suggestive of a mutual understanding. This went on for a while, and Warren must have noticed it because eventually he turned to me and said, "You're a good actor."

Later I had to be a good actor in a much larger scene between Warren and myself, and I thought everything seemed to go without a hitch. But the director, Alan Pakula, kept asking us to do it again and again. After each take Warren would go and sit next to Pakula, and they would have a quiet confab.

"Okay, let's try it again," Alan would say. And we did it again. No lines were flubbed, and everything seemed to go smoothly. I stood there after each take waiting to hear the director say, "Print it."

After about the tenth take I got tired of standing there while Warren and Alan talked, so I went and sat down.

"We were wondering how long it was gonna take you to come and sit down," one of the grips said.

We did, by my count, twenty-one takes that as far as I could see were all identical.

I had lunch with Pakula after the shooting wrapped, and I asked him what had been going on there during those many quiet discussions.

He said, "We were having an argument."

"About what?"

"I wanted Warren to become emotional. I wanted him to raise his voice in fear since the character felt his life was endangered, but he wouldn't do it. He felt his character was in control and was keeping his cool."

I wonder now if that was a requirement for being a star: never get ruffled, have every hair in place, keep your cool, and smile in the face of danger. This is not meant to be a criticism of Warren; he had plenty of messed-up hair in *Bonnie & Clyde*. And I don't remember him smiling a lot in that movie either.

The next time I heard from Warren was a few years later, when he offered me a small but important part in *Reds*, the film he was directing. I've often joked that in films I refuse to do big parts, only *small, important parts*. (*1776* was the exception.)

In *Reds* Warren wanted me to play a union leader urging several hundred members to stick together in the face of adversity. Come to think of it, I played the same role about twenty years later as president of the Screen Actors Guild.

The *Reds* shoot required me to travel to Manchester, England. The only request I made was that Bonnie accompany me. We flew to London, and the car that picked us up took us to a dreary-looking hotel. We were to take a train to Manchester, film, and then return by train to spend the night in the same dump. We dropped our bags and took the train, and when I got to the set in Manchester I corralled the line producer in the hallway of the hotel where all the important actors (e.g., Jack Nicholson, Maureen Stapleton) were staying. I started yelling at him about our poor accommodations in London. Unbeknown to me, Warren was coming down the hallway behind me. He never intruded or made his presence known, but he must have heard my rant.

While we were filming in Manchester, our luggage was moved to a two-room suite at the Dorchester Hotel in Mayfair, across from Hyde Park.

When we arrived at the Dorchester, we were informed that dinner reservations had been made for us that evening in a posh restaurant (I can't remember the name of it, but I do remember that it was across the street from MI5, the British intelligence agency). Dinner had been ordered for us. Bonnie received an orchid, and I was given a cigar. Although Warren wasn't out of pocket on our upgrades (thanks to his Paramount expense account), he certainly went out of his way for our benefit.

And he won an Oscar for directing *Reds*.

It must have been prophetic for Warren to cast me as a union leader because when I did become president of the Screen Actors

Guild and had theatrical negotiations and problems with agency contracts, I reached out to him. He was always willing to discuss the issues at length. It was important for me to get the support and energy of a major film star like Warren. I'll always be grateful to him.

In 1976, no doubt due to the country's bicentennial (though I like to believe the success of the musical and movie *1776* had something to with it), PBS aired a thirteen-episode series called *The Adams Chronicles*.

I played John Quincy Adams, John Adams's eldest son. It was a good thing that I was offered John Quincy instead of John Adams père. I'd played John Adams in *1776* for so long that I wasn't anxious to do so again, especially in a different project, so I was surprised and delighted when offered the role of his son.

As John Adams, I had argued for the abolition of slavery and tried to make that part of the Declaration of Independence. Benjamin Franklin claimed that doing so would mean the southern states wouldn't sign. Franklin won the day.

John Quincy continued his father's work on this issue, and in a widely publicized court case in New Haven in 1839 he defended a group of African captives who had been detained after staging a revolt on board the *Amistad*. (This episode of history was made into a great film by Steven Spielberg in 1997.) The key scene, however, was when John Quincy Adams argues the case in Washington when it reaches the Supreme Court.

Between my initial scenes and that climactic one, I was stricken with appendicitis—though I didn't know it. Now, most people who were filming in the New York area would likely have gone directly to a New York hospital. Not me. Knowing that something was wrong but not sure what it was, I simply got into a cab without any luggage, headed for the airport, and got on a plane home to California. Bonnie met me in Los Angeles and took me directly to my doctor, who sent me straight to the hospital, where I had my appendix removed.

My delay in seeking medical treatment was yet one more instance in which I did something that might be considered foolish, even ill advised, but in which once again luck was on my side. It reminded me of the times when I went to the wrong theater to audition but ended up getting the part anyway. This time, even though I'd put my life at stake, all turned out well. A week after surgery I was back East, ready to film my big scene in which John Quincy brings *United States v. The Amistad* before the Supreme Court.

The government gave PBS permission to film in the old Supreme Court building that had been roped off for public exhibition. During the scene I sat at the very desk Adams had used when he presented his case, trying to get the Supreme Court to address the issue of slavery. This case was argued more than twenty years before the issue tore the country apart during the Civil War.

Moving gingerly and without much strength or energy after my recent surgery, I didn't have to do much to *act* seventy-four, John Quincy's age at the time. The producers put a cot in the back of the room so I could lie down and rest between takes. According to Bonnie my "decrepitude" made the performance quite convincing; in real life Adams actually collapsed and died after making his great oration.

Several years later on an ABC show called *The Bastard* I played Samuel Adams, the hot-headed revolutionary cousin of John Adams. I have now played every important member of the Adams family, except for Abigail.

14

Home Sweet Homes

As with many actors, my ultimate success in film and TV resulted in the end of my career in the theater. It wasn't a conscious decision; it just worked out that way. I said my fond farewell to Broadway (though I didn't know it at the time) when I replaced Len Cariou in the leading role of the lawyer Egerman in *A Little Night Music,* based on a film by Ingmar Bergman, for the last six months of its New York run. I remember flying back to New York to audition for Stephen Sondheim, whom I knew briefly from *Gypsy.* After I sang he merely remarked, "You have a sweet voice." I thought that was the kiss of death, but the part was offered to me anyway. It turned out to be quite a challenge since I just had one week to rehearse and that included only a half hour with the full orchestra—at six o'clock on the very night I was to go on. Thank God for the conductor, our musical director Paul Gemignani, who in that half hour gave me a fighting chance with the tough solo opening number. *A Little Night Music* was a classy, beautifully mounted musical, and I was happy to be with it. The hard part was being away from my family for six months—and being back in New York—again!

Hal Prince was the director, and even though he had produced and directed an almost uncountable string of smash hits on Broadway over four decades, I approached the role with my own choices.

I want to make it clear that I was always professional when it came to working with directors, whether they were legendary or not. I never argued with them in public or showed them any kind of disrespect. I would listen to their notes, and internally I would make a decision whether or not to use them. But I would always nod and acknowledge the notes, as if I were going to do exactly what they said.

Such was the case with Hal Prince, who said that he didn't want me to copy Len Cariou in the role but then proceeded to give me direction that would have me doing just that. I nodded and thanked him and then did my own thing.

A week after I had started in the role Hal called a meeting of the cast and said that the show was "tighter and darker now and Bergman would be proud." This was the second time that perhaps I had pleased Bergman, but I guess I'll never know.

In 1978 a planned return to the stage was aborted. I had been scheduled to appear with the great British actress Rachel Roberts in the wild farce *Absurd Person Singular* at the Ahmanson Theatre in Los Angeles. The day we were supposed to go into rehearsal I heard from a friend that Rachel had withdrawn from the production and that she was being replaced by Eve Arden. I had agreed to do this show only because I wanted to work with Rachel Roberts, so I told the producers I was out. My name had already been printed on the posters and used in all the advance publicity, so they threatened to sue. I hired a powerful attorney who simply wrote a letter and that was the end of that. (In the letter we offered to pay for the posters, but they never took us up on it.)

My last brush with the theater was a production of A. R. Gurney's *Love Letters*. The play is very funny and touching, as it tells the story of a man and woman from the time they first meet until the death of the woman—and the story is told completely through the reading of love letters between the two. The play's "gimmick" (and I don't mean that in a negative way) was to have different celebrity couples perform the play for short runs. It was a brilliant marketing idea, and it turned into a true crowd-pleaser.

After its successful New York run in 1990 the play was set to open in Los Angeles at the intimate little jewel box known as the Canon Theatre in Beverly Hills. Bonnie and I had just come off our run on *St. Elsewhere*, and we were asked to be the first couple to perform. When I found out that there would be very little rehearsal, I said— you guessed it—no. Even though the show didn't have to be memorized (the actors hold scripts), I didn't think there was enough time to prepare. It's a lot harder than it looks to do a show like this—to be in character while constantly glancing down at the lines, then up at the audience, and not losing your place or your train of thought.

The show, by the way, was a huge hit, running for a record-breaking 565 performances, and it featured 128 different actors as the loving couple. Ben Gazzara and Gena Rowlands did it several times. So did the odd couple of Timothy Dalton with Whoopi Goldberg. The list goes on and on.

A few years later Bonnie and I finally did the show—in Buffalo for two weeks and in Santa Barbara. This time, there was time for rehearsals.

I've been offered chances to appear on Broadway again, but I've never been tempted. One offer was for the Broadway play *Morning's at Seven*. I turned it down, and the role went to my old friend Buck Henry. And I had a chance to do *Victor/Victoria* for Blake Edwards, who had directed me in the film *Blind Date*, in which I had several funny scenes with John Larroquette. Doing *Victor/Victoria* would have been a chance to star with Julie Andrews, but not even a wonderful opportunity like that could convince me to do another musical eight times per week.

There was a huge bonus to my exit from the theater and especially from New York: I got to spend a lot of time with our boys, especially during the early days when we first moved to Studio City and I wasn't working very much in TV and film.

I became adept at carpooling and especially at cooking—I love feeding people. I had always dreamed of a "domestic" lifestyle, and that dream had finally come true.

When we lived in New York and I was doing *1776*, I had little time with my family; there were shows every day, a matinee on Saturday, and performances on every holiday, including Christmas. Robert didn't like to go to the theater, but occasionally Michael would come (he was older), and I think that's where he probably fell in love with singing and performing.

I think Michael thought of me more as John Adams than as his father. I remember once when I was explaining to him that John Adams had a son who also became president, he said, "Who, *me?*" Michael was very smart from an early age—he was skipped ahead a grade—and he fit in with the older kids because he was mature and very tall. He was always outgoing and quick to make friends—an "all-American" boy. (Later he would graduate from UCLA and get his master's in music at USC.) Michael continues to perform, singing with opera companies, and he also teaches English as a second language at UCLA.

Robert, from the beginning, was totally different from Michael, which is not unusual for siblings from separate adoptions.

Robert was always much more private, slow to socialize at school or with a group, as is often the case with children who are very bright. Bonnie and I were his primary companions, and I fondly remember the many hours we would spend in the pool together, both in Connecticut and in Studio City. One problem, which we didn't figure out until years later—not even the doctors in New York picked up on it—was that he had no peripheral vision. (Fortunately, doctors at the Jule Styne Eye Institute at UCLA finally diagnosed it.) He was wildly creative and spent much of his childhood in his room with art and building projects. When he was older, he was accepted at Wesleyan University because of an outstanding essay he wrote comparing the state of his room to an M. C. Escher lithograph, *Order and Chaos*. (Escher said, "We adore chaos because we love to produce order.") The premise: what looked like a total disaster in his room was actually a meticulously planned and executed arrangement of forms. The kid was deep.

Robert, like his brother, was not only a gifted artist but also an amazing musician—he could sit down and play the piano beautifully—but unlike Michael he was not a performer. He's now a front-end web developer, thus utilizing his artistic background. His practically perfect memory makes him an excellent troubleshooter.

After we moved to Studio City I was home most of the time with the boys, and even when we did *St. Elsewhere* Bonnie and I had working hours that were as normal as those of any parents, and we always had the weekends free. It was heaven.

John Cleese was once asked if Santa Barbara was heaven, and he said, "No, but it's the same zip code."

Bonnie and I would occasionally spend a weekend at a motel

down at the beach in Santa Barbara while my parents came over to the house to keep an eye on our two boys, who were only eight and ten at the time. (They were very good grandparents, and the boys loved them.)

Later, with the work in television that came along and the money that came with it, we began to think of a second place—an escape— perhaps a beach house in Oxnard or Ventura, but what we saw in those places didn't suit us. The homes in Ventura Keys were arranged alongside a canal built for small boats. Back porches faced the homes across the canal not more than thirty or forty feet away—I could imagine a neighbor across the way yelling, "Saw your show last night"—with a thumbs-down gesture. No, that wouldn't do.

"I think you'd be happier in Santa Barbara," our real estate agent said.

So off we went to Montecito, in Santa Barbara County, where the tree-lined streets reminded us of Connecticut. We looked at properties in the area for almost a year. There was one house just off East Valley Road that we fell in love with, but it was too expensive. We kept looking, but we couldn't get that house out of our minds. Whatever else we saw didn't quite compare. Then, suddenly, the price on our first choice went down and we grabbed it.

After months of renovations, it was official. We had a second California home. Thus began a routine that, schedule permitting, meant leaving Studio City on Friday mornings and spending a long weekend in Santa Barbara. We've been doing that for more than twenty-five years.

In the 1970s when I was on *McCloud*, in an episode called "The Day New York Turned Blue," I did a couple of scenes with a young Bernadette Peters, who of course later became a major Broadway star. The scenes were about mistaken identity and turned out to be very amusing. The scenes must have stuck in *McCloud* producer Glen Larson's mind because six years later I got a call from him while I was working on *St. Elsewhere*. He explained that he was taking a show idea to New York to pitch to the networks, and he had a few lines he needed an actor to record. Would I do him the favor of going over to Universal Studios to do the lines? I said sure and went into a recording room where Glen handed me the pages of dialogue I was to record. I scanned them and looked up.

"This is the voice of a car?" I asked, incredulous.

He nodded.

In the mid-1960s I'd once had an interview meeting with the author/producer of a show called *My Mother the Car*. That meeting left him so depressed he almost dropped the idea of doing the show (which, in my opinion, would have been a good idea).

I didn't want to do the same thing to Glen Larson, so I sighed and said, "Okay, let's do it."

"You might do it as a robot," the casting director said.

"No," I said.

I began, but Glen interrupted.

"Why don't you do it like a Ma Bell telephone operator?"

"No, just let me finish recording it, okay?"

I wanted to get it over with, so I continued in my own voice, which turned out to be the best way to go. Not that I'd given it much thought. I just wanted to finish it.

"Thank you," Glen said.

"You're welcome. Goodbye."

I left the lot and promptly forgot the whole episode. Three or four weeks later I had a call from Glen saying the show, called *Knight Rider*, had been picked up by NBC and would I do the voice of KITT, the car. KITT was an acronym for Knight Industries Two Thousand. I told Glen I didn't know how I could, since I already had a starring role on *St. Elsewhere*.

"We'll be on the same network, NBC. They've said it's all right with them, and we'll work it out. We'll record each show at your convenience."

How could I turn that down? I had my agent insist on my receiving no billing. No one would know. It would be another *Battlestar Galactica* experience as Norman the Clown.

The day after *Knight Rider* premiered I was taking a walk in my neighborhood when a stranger standing on his lawn on the other side of the street yelled, "Hey, congratulations on your new show!"

How the heck had he figured it out? I mumbled some kind of acknowledgment that I hope I managed to combine with a note of gratitude and hurried on.

Apparently I was the last to know that my voice was such a signature feature of the show—there was no hiding. *Knight Rider* became a hit, and KITT the car was a big part of it. How many times could I be so wrong about the parts I stumbled into?

After all these years mail still comes in for KITT every week; I've signed pictures of the car, numerous license plates, and even a fender.

Once, at a celebrity-signing event in a huge marketing tent outside London, Bonnie and I were signing photographs when a well-dressed, middle-aged gentleman handed me a picture of the car to sign.

"Excuse me," he said as I put pen to picture.

"Yes?"

"When you are KITT, where are you in the car?"

I looked up at his face to see if he was serious. Not a glimmer of mockery.

"You mean, was I under the hood or in the trunk?" I asked.

He nodded, eyes wide.

"Well, actually I'm in a soundproof recording room talking into a microphone."

"Oh," he said, a tad crestfallen. He took his picture and walked away. A big part of me wished I had told him that they had squeezed me under the dashboard.

Call them frames of mind, or moods, if you will, but they come with their own dispositions, behavior patterns, habits, and histories. Many of these "self states" are created in early childhood experiences. My current psychologist, Dr. Shane, insists I was an abused child, robbed of a normal childhood, put into situations (performing) that I had no control over, and left unable to express my anger, my fears, and my dread of knowing what was expected of me in the future. Along with those negative aspects of my childhood came no sense of accomplishment, no rewards, no compliments, no words of encouragement; I never remember hearing "good job" or "well done" or "you did good," which surely children need to hear. Instead, I heard that we shouldn't get "swelled heads" (my mother's words).

Her life in show business didn't become a reality until she had children. She lived her dreams—her robust dreams—through me and my sisters.

When my mother was ill and dying (with my dad caring for her at their home in Pacoima), I went to see her. It was just after I had won my first Emmy Award.

"Well, your son is now a TV star," I said.

She lifted her head from the pillow and in her weak, croaking voice she said, "Big *Broadway* star."

Those were the last words she ever said to me.

It sometimes happens when you're lucky enough to have a leading role on a successful TV show, as I was on *St. Elsewhere*, that the audience's familiarity with you becomes attractive to advertisers who want to connect you to their product. Their offers for your services in television commercials can be very lucrative. Bonnie and I, playing husband and wife on *St. Elsewhere*, did a commercial playing husband and wife for the product I Can't Believe It's Not Butter—a rather long name—but the product is still on your grocer's shelves. And we still use it.

I did one spot playing a hard-assed manager ruling over things at Hughes Markets. The video spots were okay by me, but then, for an added stipend, I allowed them to put up full-length, larger-than-life size cardboard cutouts of me in all the Hughes Markets. That did it! No matter where I went, whether to the corner grocer, to a Ralphs market, or just about any parking lot, I heard, "Saw you at Hughes!" or "What are you doing here? You're supposed to be at Hughes!" or "Aha! Caught you. Wait 'til I tell Hughes." It became unbearable. For a person who cherished his anonymity (granted, I'm in the wrong business for that), what a foolish situation to be in. So I ended it, without actually planning to. When I was being interviewed on a radio show, Hughes was mentioned. I simply said, "I shop at Gelson's." My Hughes commercial was dropped the next day.

With *St. Elsewhere* and *Knight Rider* running at the same time, I was advised to "incorporate" for financial reasons, so Bonnie and I went off to a lawyer's office. I've never been business-minded in any way—Bonnie has always taken care of all that—so the lawyer spoke directly to her while I sat quietly smoking a pipe (a terrible habit I had for about ten years).

When it was clear to the lawyer that we needed to have everything under Bonnie's control (since she understood it all), he said to me, "You know the way this is set up, Bonnie could take a lover and give him all your money."

I said, "Well, she might take a lover, but I guarantee you she'd never give him a nickel."

15

Boy Oh Boy

Over the years you fine-tune your acting ability. It doesn't mean you're not capable of giving a lousy performance now and again, but on the whole you reach a point where you've increased your level of achievement. And it's at that point, assuming that you are financially secure, that you have to protect your reputation by choosing carefully the roles you commit to. It was with that in mind that I expressed my doubts about taking on the role of George Feeny in a half-hour sitcom called *Boy Meets World*. At a meeting with the show's author and executive producer, Michael Jacobs, already an established playwright and sitcom creator, as well as a movie producer, I told him I didn't want to play a high school teacher who's made to look foolish for the sake of some cheap laughs. I had too much respect for the underpaid, underappreciated teachers of this country to portray one of them as a fool. Michael told me about Bob Stevens, a Shakespeare-loving high school drama teacher he had had back in New Jersey who was his mentor and a man he greatly respected. With this teacher as his inspiration, he created George Feeny. Michael was very persuasive and assured me that he would never have me play an idiot, so I came on board.

Michael wanted a strong-willed older man in the cast for comic tension and depth, someone like his high school teacher. From the beginning, he told me, he thought of me because he had liked my work in *The Graduate*, *Two for the Road*, and *1776*. He had never met me before, but he told me that he could see that I played formidable characters with an edge and a humanity that appealed to him.

He likes to tell the story about how after the table read of our first show I went to his office and quit. I wasn't aware at the time that the series was in flux—that it hadn't yet found its own voice, its own point of view. Michael was in the middle of a rewrite as we spoke and asked me to give him twenty-four hours to complete it. If I felt the same way after I read it, he said, then I could leave. The new script had me deliver to my student, Cory, the facts of life, tying it into the importance of Shakespeare's *Romeo and Juliet*, which my student was studying and hated: "I live on the other side of the fence from you, Cory. It's impossible not to face in your direction every once in a while and notice the people in the next yard. And through the years as I've gotten to know them, it is apparent they are fine individuals. But, their real strength comes from being a family. And do you know why they are a family, Cory? Because at one time a man and a woman realized that they loved each other and pursued the unlimited potential of what may come from that love, and here you are. There is no greater aspiration than to have love in our lives, Mr. Matthews. Romeo knew it and died for it."

Here was a Mr. Feeny I knew I could play. I called Michael and said, "If this is what you can do in twelve hours, I will never quit again."

And that was the beginning of the longest series with which I've ever been involved, a seven-season run, from 1993 to 2000. Reruns of the show are still on TV. Memories of it fill the Internet. Blog posts dedicated to Mr. Feeny are common. Young people calling me by that name still stop me on the street or come up to me in restaurants. Once in New York I felt a little bit like the Beatles as a group of yeshiva boys chased me out of a Broadway theater while shouting "Feeny!" and thus forcing me to abandon my family temporarily and escape by running around the block.

I don't care for most television sitcoms. I rarely watch them. (I do love *Seinfeld*, though, especially the physical comedy of Julia Louis-Dreyfus.) Apparently I'm not alone, as the ones I'd done in the past, like *Captain Nice*, died quickly from lack of an audience.

After *St. Elsewhere* I had been offered numerous sitcoms, mostly with roles for both Bonnie and me as a couple. It was strange. We had played a couple in an hour-long *drama*, but the gods of show business somehow had decided we needed to be in a *comedy* together. One of the shows we turned down, *Empty Nest*, turned out to be a huge hit for NBC but only after an extensive rewrite that also rei-magined the entire concept of the show.

You can imagine my surprise when *Boy Meets World* was not only a big success but one that created such an indelible impression on an entire generation more than half a century younger than me.

Mr. Feeny's appeal was due to the fact that he was a friend, a mentor, and an advisor all rolled into one. In a stroke of creative genius Michael even made Mr. Feeny a neighbor. At first this plot point got on my nerves. "How long am I going to have to be talking to people across this back fence?" I said to him that first season, pointing to the waist-high white picket fence that separated the Feeny home from the Matthews home on the set. "The way this is going," Michael replied, "I can't see us lasting more than seven years."

Feeny never "talked down" to the kids in the show, and the writing always assumed that the audience was intelligent enough to get the comedy. As the old saying goes, "If you have to explain the joke, it isn't funny." And that's why it still holds up in reruns. *Boy Meets World* is funny, *genuinely* funny.

I still get fan mail to this day from (now-grown) fans who tell me how important the show and the role I played were to them in their formative years. And Mr. Feeny's impact on popular culture shows up in social media, such as the Buzzfeed post "16 Things Mr. Feeny Taught Us," featuring clips in which I say things like, "If you let people's perception of you dictate your behavior, you will never grow as a person." Even parents have thanked me for the part I played in a show they felt comfortable having their children watch.

The show became a hit very quickly, helped in part by the scheduling. By creating a block of kid-oriented comedies on Friday night, when there was no competition from school homework, ABC pulled whole families to the network. The ABC executives called it "couch programming." They thought that children would react positively to the new shows and drag their parents with them. They were right.

That doesn't mean they were right about everything, and ABC followed the usual network pattern of interfering in the show's creative process. Michael loved making references to literature and the wider world in his scripts, but network executives didn't always catch on or, if they did, they doubted that viewers would. An ABC executive told Michael the Shakespeare references in the script for the pilot were "too intricate." The audience would not relate to them. Michael was forced to take them out. The executive who had ordered him to remove the *Romeo and Juliet* lines complained afterward that now the script didn't work. "What happened?" the executive asked. Michael replied, "You happened."

Through the seven years of episodes, my character followed Cory (played by Ben Savage), his family, and his friends as their lives changed. Mr. Feeny began the series as Cory's middle school teacher, later became his high school principal, and at the end was his college professor. (I've been told that fans who were following the show were distraught every time the kids graduated, fearing that it would be the end of Mr. Feeny.) As the show's child actors grew older and romantic plot lines became more common—particularly Cory's on-again, off-again relationship with Topanga Lawrence, played by Danielle Fishel—the share of female viewers between the ages of seventeen and thirty-five soared.

And Feeny became the pivot point for the show's budding relationships. The emotional growth of the characters relied on his advice about love, college, marriage, and life.

For me this show was a huge change from playing Dr. Mark Craig on *St. Elsewhere*. Dr. Craig was never the sort of man from whom young people sought warm counsel. That sort of advice seemed foreign coming out of me, but Michael explained that was exactly why he wanted me in the role. The combination of prickly rectitude and fatherly concern was irresistible to viewers, he said. As the part grew and Feeny's words took hold for a generation, I began to see what he meant.

Having Feeny as both neighbor and teacher, and later as school principal and college professor, kept me on the screen much of the time. If Feeny wasn't simultaneously infuriating and counseling the kids at John Adams (!) Middle School and High School, he was doing the same to the Matthews family next door, which included Cory, his brother Eric (played by Will Friedle), their little sister Morgan (Lindsay Ridgeway and Lily Nicksay), and their parents, Alan and Amy (William Russ and Betsy Randle), as well as Cory's best friend, Shawn Hunter (Rider Strong).

Michael Jacobs had assembled a talented young cast, and over the years they developed into real pros with exceptional comic timing. I don't know if I had anything to do with any of that growth, but Will Friedle has told me that I taught them by example, which was the way that Howard Lindsay had taught me all those years ago during *Life with Father*.

They were good kids, and they had good parents. They didn't know that I had been a child actor myself. I shared no stories about my days in radio or on Broadway. That wasn't my place. I treated them as fellow professionals, just as I had the adult actors I worked with on other shows.

I enjoyed watching the young cast members grow up. Ben Savage was eleven when we started working together. By the time the show ended he was seventeen and driving a truck into the studio parking lot. I thought the cast and their families learned to handle the hard work and pressure well. I was very careful not to take an advisory role. Bonnie suggested I give the young actors some tips, but I wouldn't do it. They did their own thing, and I did my own thing. I wanted it to remain a working relationship of equals.

There was a family feeling on that set. Michael was a kind man, very religious and very warm. Bonnie and I made friends with the adult actors, particularly William Russ, whom everyone called Rusty, and Betsy Randle. When we first went out to dinner, Rusty too said he was surprised to find himself doing a sitcom, having had a long career as a dramatic actor. "I only did it because you were in it," he said.

Having said all that, I must confess that performing in *Boy Meets World* presented certain difficulties for me, and in seven years I was never quite comfortable. We rehearsed for four days a week, and during that time the staff and the cast made the set a delight. But the days we taped the show the studio became a circus. It was a three-camera show with a live audience brought in to provide authentic laughter rather than the canned laughter many shows used (and abused). The audience consisted mostly of noisy young people who were there to have a good time. That would have been fine, except that the audience was encouraged to be "over the top." Like most three-camera sitcoms, there was a comedian on the set to "warm up" the audience with a few jokes and then instruct them that they were there to *laugh*. (Not much had changed in TV since I was a professional laugher during *Mister Peepers*.) During the taping they laughed on every other line of dialogue, or so it seemed to me. You never knew when they were going to laugh; sometimes they'd laugh before you got to the funny line. And when I'd flub a line they'd laugh like hell, but I'd be miserable. These audiences loved to see the actors mess up; I never understood why. Perhaps they enjoyed being in on a sort of inside joke.

Then there was what I can only call a "party" in back of the sets— friends and family of our own young actors, all milling about and munching on food laid out on a long table. Their chattering only stopped when the assistant director yelled, "Rolling!" This environment was no place for me, so I simply hid in my dressing room until it was time to do my scenes. But even then the commotion of moving cameras, laughter, and other noise made it difficult for this old man to concentrate (I was sixty-five when the series began). I'm very old school, and I need a short moment of calm before I make my entrance. There was no understanding of this on the set, and that's why someone didn't hesitate to inform me just before an entrance one day that he was sorry to hear that Ed Flanders had committed suicide. Ed was my Emmy-winning costar on *St. Elsewhere* and quite honestly my favorite scene partner of all time. I absolutely adored working with him and was devastated by the news. For the first (and only) time I couldn't make my entrance, not for a while anyway.

I only "lost it" once. We were on location, inside a building with some musical equipment. Michael was there keeping an eye on things as he sat at a piano. The younger cast members were still learning how to handle the demands of a weekly show. It had been a long day. Their attention spans had expired. They were blowing off steam.

The noise wouldn't stop. I decided I had had it and shouted very loudly, "Everyone be quiet!!"

They immediately sat down and went silent. Michael said the young actors were in awe of me but knew little about me. They had no clue that I was similar to them in some ways, having also been a child performer. They were so ignorant of the real me that they thought I was British, he said. He claimed even he caught an occasional hint of an English accent in my performance, including the impromptu one I delivered to the young actors that day.

"I don't care what the script says," I said. "I don't care what the blocking is. I don't care if you have made some mistakes in your lines. What I do care about is that your heads are in the game. Your heads are *not* in this game, and *I will not have it!!*"

The speech lasted less than a minute. Then I left. I passed Michael as he sat at the piano. Like everyone else, he looked stunned. The cast had seen me blow up many times, but only as Mr. Feeny delivering his lines. Michael said he knew I was not really angry, just frustrated. He also heard in my speech the rhythms of another character I had played years before.

As I stomped past him, he put his hands on the piano keys and played the first few bars of the theme to *St. Elsewhere*, one of the most recognizable melodies ever written for series television. He was not sure how I would react. But I got the message from him—he knew that I was "performing." The kids couldn't see my face. I smiled and winked at Michael. I turned to give my young colleagues another stern look, then made my exit.

After seven years *Boy Meets World* ended—just as Michael had predicted. I felt close to my fellow actors. Toward the end, when the main characters had reached college, Bonnie was cast as a dean and became a love interest for Feeny, then a professor. Our characters married on the show, perhaps to reassure viewers that Mr. Feeny would not be too lonely now that the students who had occupied so much of his time were graduating from college and moving to New York City.

Many fans of the show have told me they cried at the last scene of the last episode, when my four favorite students said goodbye to me. The episode was full of flashbacks to early episodes, when the actors had all been middle school age, not the three robust young men and the young woman who now appeared on the screen. For the last scene the four of them ask Mr. Feeny to meet them in their old middle school classroom, where it all started.

"We wanted to know if you have anything else to teach us," Topanga said.

"My work with you is done," I said.

"I don't know," said Shawn. "It's pretty scary. Going off to a whole new world."

"You're ready to go into that world."

"Even me?" asked Eric.

"Even you," I said.

I paused for a moment, then sat at a corner of my desk and delivered a favorite Mr. Feeny slogan that has since gone "viral," as they say: "Believe in yourselves. Dream. Try. Do Good."

"Don't you mean do well?" asked Topanga, by far the best student in the group.

"No, I mean do *good*."

"Well, I guess there is just one thing left then," Eric said. "Tell us you love us."

I bristled. "Now look," I said. "If there's one thing I've taught you, it is there is a line between teacher and student that must never be crossed."

"Tell us you love us," Eric repeated.

"I regard all my students equally."

"Oh, you know we're your favorites," said Shawn.

"Come on, Feeny," said Cory. "You haven't even talked to another student for seven years."

That was a funny line, a wink at the audience members who knew that no *Boy Meets World* episode had ever shown me spending much time with anyone but those four. I hugged each of them. They left the classroom one by one, leaving me with Cory, my young friend Ben Savage, the star of the show, his name always appearing just before mine in the credits.

"You coming with us, Mr. Feeny?" he asked. "You gonna sneak up on us in Central Park or something?"

"No. I will remain here."

"You'll always be with us. As long as we live, okay?"

I nodded. Ben walked out of the classroom. After he left I reached down and touched one of the little middle school desks in the front row. I was the last person on the screen at the end of *Boy Meets World*.

"I love you all," I said softly. "Class dismissed."

16

Mr. President

It started out innocently enough: Kathleen Haigney, a professional ballet dancer and union activist in Bonnie's three-times-a-week ballet class, asked Bonnie if she would be interested in running for president of the Screen Actors Guild.

"Hell, no," Bonnie said.

"How about Bill?" Kathleen asked.

"Double hell no."

It might have ended there, but later Kathleen called to ask if we would take a meeting with a group of concerned performers to help them find a well-known actor to run against SAG president Richard Masur, who was seeking an unprecedented third term. He had spent a number of years as a successful working actor, but I think he considered being SAG president his greatest role. Over the years the SAG presidency has always been won by a celebrity. Sometimes it was a big star from the movies—like James Cagney or Charlton Heston. Sometimes it was an iconic star from TV—like Ed Asner. And sometimes, just someone who had worked a lot and was a familiar face—like Kathleen Nolan or, as I mentioned, Richard Masur.

We agreed to meet at Art's Deli ("Where every sandwich is a work of Art!") in Studio City. Art's is a favorite haunt, not just of mine but of the television crowd that works and lives in the area. When Bonnie and I arrived, four actors I had never met before proceeded to tell us about the many dire situations that existed at the guild. They told me that the SAG National Board was a war zone—that there was a political battle between Los Angeles actors and actors in the rest of the country, especially New York. Most of the work in the country was in LA, and actors in "branches" of the union around the country were resentful and eager to make concessions to employers to attract more work to their areas.

The four actors also explained that the union was being run not by actors but by the paid staff, who were making arbitrary decisions that weren't benefiting the actors they were hired to represent. This was in spite of the fact that many of these staff members, as I was to find out, had six-figure salaries.

If this sounds like a microcosm of the bigger political picture in this country—Congress made ineffectual by infighting and useless overpaid government bureaucrats filling important jobs—you'd be right. A union, however, by its very nature cannot function unless there is solidarity, especially during a strike or the threat of a strike. My learning curve about SAG had begun as I found out that the union had become completely dysfunctional.

The four actors at Art's Deli—Chuck Sloan, Bob Carlson, David Jolliffe, and Paul Napier—zeroed in on the plight of the commercial actor. A very small percentage of actors had ever made a living with acting, but now even the successful ones—those lucky enough to have carved out a career in commercials—were suddenly in trouble due to the explosion of cable networks (USA, ESPN, etc.) Advertisers were making a lot of commercials for cable, and that sounds like a good thing—more work for actors, right? But there is an important caveat in the world of commercials: if you appear in a commercial for Pepsi, you can't do one for Coke. That makes total sense, but if your commercial is running on one of the broadcast networks—CBS, NBC, ABC, et cetera—you are compensated for this exclusivity; you receive a residual payment *every* time that commercial runs. For those of you who don't know, only the biggest movie and TV stars make their living from their initial contracts. Everyone else makes the bulk of their living afterward, from residual payments generated by reruns. Most actors work so infrequently that without residual payments they would be unable to stay in the business and keep pursuing further work.

Residual payments are despised by producers and studios, but they actually work to their benefit. As long as there are residuals, there will always be a pool of talented actors waiting in the wings to be hired. Without residuals, most actors would completely leave "the business," and producers would be forced to find nonprofessionals out there, in other lines of work, who may or may not have talent and who might not be willing to quit their day jobs for a small part here and there.

On cable, however, under the contract at the time, the residuals were abysmal—you were paid a maximum of only $11.32 per day (during which the cable network could run your commercial an unlimited number of times). If you watch cable TV, you know that they run some commercials over and over again at every commercial break every day for weeks or months. This creates overexposure, and it can doom an actor in commercials. Advertisers don't want to hire actors who are too closely associated with *one* product. So imagine—you get a commercial on a cable network for Ford, so you can't work for any other car company, and Coke doesn't want to hire you because "that's the guy from the Ford commercial—I'm tired of seeing him."

Chuck, Bob, David, and Paul described how established actors—earning only eleven bucks per day—were losing their health insurance, facing mounting debt, even losing their homes. They threw so many facts and stories at me I could barely absorb it all.

I began to think about how fortunate I was not to be in their situation, how lucky I had been in my career. Here I was coming to the end of the seventh season of my third successful TV series. I'd been employed almost continuously for the last twenty years. The actors sitting with me at Art's were all younger than I was, still struggling to make a living (or hang on to a living), and they were looking for a candidate who would replace the current president (and his regime) and try to truly make a difference.

Without much thought at all I found myself saying, "How about me running?" Dead silence. They weren't expecting that, since Bonnie had already told Kathleen that I would say "double hell no." "I don't know if I'd be able to win," I added.

"You'd win in a second," Chuck said.

Now remember, I had been in the army, and the first thing you learn there is to never volunteer for anything. But here I was blithely volunteering to step into the great unknown. Up to this point I'd been in the SAG Hollywood offices only once, years ago, to attend the memorial of a departed friend. I had no idea what I was getting myself into. The only time I was a union leader was that one role in the movie *Reds*. And in the movies, there's always a clear depiction of the good guys and the bad guys—you see people like Sally Field in *Norma Rae*, risking her life to stand up to the corrupt and evil employers. You see coal miners standing shoulder to shoulder, bathed in the light of brotherhood.

Well, that's the movies. In real life—during my two-year presidency—I was instead shown the absolute worst side of people, who turned out to be utterly duplicitous, treacherous, and vindictive. And I'm not talking about "evil employers"—I'm talking about my fellow actors who were so bent on retaining control of the National Board and regaining control over the presidency of the union that they eventually destroyed the union itself. It was a case of "we have met the enemy and they are us."

But I also made lifelong friendships with a number of fellow actors who had already been working tirelessly and selflessly for many years at the union (for years before I got there) and would continue to do so after I was gone. These were people like Scott Wilson, who has had a long career and recent success on *The Walking Dead*.

I was entering the race late, but a group of actors had come forward calling themselves the Performers Alliance, and they passed me from handler to handler, taking me from one location to another where actors congregated, and I collected hundreds of signatures at the last minute to qualify for the ballot. It must have been a huge shock to Richard Masur, who thought that he was running for his third term unopposed. There was animosity from his camp after I was elected—that was understandable, coming from the losing side—but I was shocked to see the open hostility from the paid staff.

The national executive director (or NED, who is like the CEO of the union) was immediately withdrawn and uncooperative when I came on the scene. (He was a close friend of Richard Masur.) The NED never came into my office nor did he ever offer me a single word of advice. No one on his staff ever offered me assistance of any kind. And here I was slated to lead the negotiations for the two biggest union contracts—the commercials contract and the TV/theatrical contract (covering movies and most network TV).

And so it was in this atmosphere that I began two of the most horrendous years of my life. I was clearly under siege—not from employers outside the SAG building but from supposed brothers and sisters *within*.

My first duty was to chair a National Board meeting. This one was held in a huge meeting room atop the Sheraton Universal Hotel. The room was filled with long tables facing another long table up on a dais. Seated at the tables were 107 National Board members from all over the country. The elevator opened directly into the room, and I felt like a hapless Christian about to enter the Roman Coliseum. There was a roar from the crowd. Could it be for me? No, it was just the "lions" as they sat in their "cages." As I was escorted to the dais, they became hushed and stared at me. I sat down and smiled—they continued to stare. At my table sat our legal counsel, recording secretary, vice president, NED, and two women whose jobs were a mystery to me. In fact the whole thing was a mystery to me—did I actually rap the gavel and bring the meeting to order?

A chubby gentleman stood in front of a floor microphone and began a litany of grievances at the top of his lungs. These were all in reference to past motions of the National Board. The harangue went on for ten minutes, and since this was all regarding things that happened before I was elected, I didn't have a clue as to what he was talking about. He ended with a great flourish of the papers in his hand and walked off the floor. Not knowing what to do, I simply said, "Well, there you are." The whole room roared with laughter. Startled by this, I looked around the room and saw the chubby orator on the sidelines grinning and throwing kisses at me. Was he trying to say there were no hard feelings? What on earth was this all about? There was no time to find out because there were already actors lined up at microphones at the front and back of the room, awaiting their turn to speak.

The dramatic speeches continued. *Friends, Romans, country-men*—or words to that effect. I did not recognize many of the speakers—I couldn't help wondering if any of them had acting jobs. Maybe for some their last job was a long time ago and this was their only chance to perform again in front of an audience.

On my second visit to the SAG offices, on Wilshire Boulevard, I was introduced to the staff, each coming out of individual offices to shake my hand. No one told me what their job entailed or how they could help me in the upcoming negotiations. There was a definite sense that the staff had circled the wagons out of loyalty to Richard Masur. There were some good people there I'm sure, but there was also a culture of unchecked corruption. I found out later that during the previous administration staff members had even gone so far as to stuff ballot boxes in a well-documented case that was buried by the National Board.

The only person who appeared to be on my side (and the best thing that happened to me) was my secretary, Nadia, who proved to be a godsend. Having served as Masur's secretary, she was able to explain what was expected of me in all my presidential duties, and she also was able to protect me against hostile phone calls and intrusions into my office (and there were plenty of them).

I was inexperienced and unprepared, to be sure, but I had some personal strengths that the membership hadn't seen in their president for a very long time. I was quoted as saying, "I'm not afraid of anyone in Hollywood"—a bit of braggadocio that immediately hit the trade papers. As Bill Daniels I could speak my mind; as SAG president I realized that I had to be careful about what I said.

I hadn't seen Kirk Douglas for many years, but I was certainly happy to see him when he reached out after my election and asked to speak at the SAG national membership meeting. He got up and made a tremendous speech in front of hundreds of members about the importance of our union and the uniqueness of it—nowhere else could you find a membership where there was such a large disparity in income. And it was the responsibility of the highest earners, he said, to take care of those at the bottom who needed it most. Unfortunately for us, our employers would see things differently.

Before we even began the commercials contract negotiations the commercial employers, represented by the Joint Policy Committee (JPC), sent SAG a letter stating that Class A residuals had to come to an end. (Class A residuals are the ones paid on network TV and are the lifeblood of every commercial actor.) Remember that this was before negotiations had even begun. Was it just a warning shot? It wasn't, as it turns out. They meant business. As negotiations got under way and we tried to get an increase in cable residuals, they kept insisting on doing away with the formula for Class A. If we had agreed to this approach, it would have been the same as taking money out of one of your pockets and putting it into another. A lot of pain and no gain.

The JPC would not budge, and so the board of directors *unanimously* voted to strike. Unfortunately for actors, anything worth fighting for has been won only through a strike. That's a historical fact, as seen in 1956, 1960, 1978, 1980, 1987, and 1988. Without those strikes there would be no residuals paid for anything. There would be no pension and health plan. Sometimes just the threat of a strike has been enough to gain at least a fair contract. But not this time. The JPC was determined to force us into an unconditional surrender.

The commercials strike of 2000 lasted for six months and was the longest strike in the history of the union. It could have been much shorter if it hadn't been for a few devastating developments.

As I said, solidarity is everything, and in the beginning even the New York branch members, who were so vociferously anti-Hollywood in the boardroom, stepped up and worked their butts off, organizing picketing. This was true in all the branches.

But as the strike wore on, the actors who were no longer in power at the union began to turn on us and play the blame game: "This would never have happened under Richard Masur!"

The anti–Bill Daniels camp managed to organize a pretty good-sized rebellion. Supposedly secret but well-attended meetings were held to protest the strike and to find solutions that would bring the strike to an end. You can be sure that the JPC knew about these meetings—there are no secrets in Hollywood—and there is no doubt that the meetings did nothing but help prolong the strike, with the JPC gleefully waiting to divide and conquer as the actors turned on one another.

But give credit to the National Board, which voted unanimously to stay on strike not once but *twice* during the six-month ordeal. In spite of all the political posturing, they knew what was at stake.

At the very beginning of the strike our strategy was to create a national boycott against one or more of the biggest advertisers. The chief negotiator and other executives were adamantly opposed to this idea—they said a boycott wouldn't work. But how did they know that, especially since, as it turned out, they didn't know any better?

Finally we went over the head of the chief negotiator and called press conferences where we called for a boycott against Procter & Gamble, the makers of soap, toothpaste, and many of the things that you see on TV commercials. (P&G, by the way, was also one of the earliest sponsors of TV shows, hence the nickname "*soap* opera" for daytime dramas.)

We had high-profile actors such as Susan Sarandon, Treat Williams, Richard Dreyfus, Julia Roberts, and Rosie O'Donnell there, all of whom spoke with passion about the unfairness of the commercials contract when it came to the average actor. They were heroes during all of this—they had nothing to win and everything to lose. (They ran the risk of advertisers in the future potentially refusing to hire them for multimillion-dollar commercial campaigns.)

The executives at SAG were actually *against* the inclusion of famous people—they felt it reduced public sympathy for the cause by creating the impression that millionaires (not struggling working people) were on strike. I ignored the staff and brought in many stars, such as Elliott Gould, who worked diligently to bring in many other celebrity actors to help our cause. And then there was Kevin Spacey, who turned out to be a great asset—literally. Kevin led the way, and soon Helen Hunt, Harrison Ford, Nicolas Cage, and others had donated millions of dollars to striking actors through the SAG Foundation to help them pay bills and buy groceries.

The strike finally ended when Bonnie, Rob Schneider, and a small group of actors (including my old friend from *The Zoo Story*, Peter Mark Richman) went to Cincinnati and disrupted the Procter & Gamble stockholders meeting. (They didn't crash the meeting—

they had cleverly gotten proxies from stockholders, so they were attending the meeting legally.)

Our group got up in the meeting and began making speeches about the toll that the strike was taking on actors and their families. The CEO, Mr. Pepper (love that name!), told them he would meet with them after the stockholders meeting if they would simply be quiet.

Mr. Pepper kept his word and met with Bonnie and Rob. Bonnie introduced herself by saying, "Do you remember me? I was the first 'Pampers Mom.'" They had a nice chat, and then the conversation turned to the strike and the boycott. Mr. Pepper asked, "Why are you doing this to us? We're a business." Rob replied, "So are we." Mr. Pepper then said that the strike would be over within one week. And it was.

Had we been allowed to implement the boycott on Procter & Gamble at the very beginning of the strike we would have gotten the attention of Mr. Pepper and perhaps all the CEOs of all the companies who relied on actors for their advertising. The strike would never have lasted as long as it did. It appears now that lawyers and ad agencies were really the driving force behind the JPC's intransigence and that the advertisers themselves (like Mr. Pepper) didn't really understand what it was all about.

The day after the strike ended, Richard Masur declared on National Public Radio that "in a strike no one wins."

Really? Actors received a 140 percent raise in cable residuals. To understand the magnitude of this kind of achievement, no union contract negotiated before or since has gotten more than a 3 percent gain per year. We also gained jurisdiction over commercials in the area of new media (and at the time few people could envision what the hell that meant). As an explosion of commercials on the Internet was about to begin, we had clearly insured the future. And we insured the present (and the future) by preserving Class A residuals on network TV.

The total amount paid to actors in the commercials contract has grown practically every year since, breaking records. In 2014 the total amount paid to commercial actors topped $1 billion. We would never have reached that figure without the gains of the 2000 strike.

The strike was so successful that when it came time to negotiate the TV/theatrical contract, Lew Wasserman—the last link to Jack Warner, Louis B. Mayer, and the other moguls from the golden age of Hollywood—asked me to come to his office at Universal Studios. He insisted I call him Lew, and without ever mentioning the commercials strike he proceeded to give me his sage advice. He said, "Bill, I have a studio here with a lot of soundstages that I have to keep busy, and I can't do it without actors to work in them. And of course actors need to make a living. So in fact we need each other. We are in fact partners. Sometimes we don't give the actors enough, and we have to fix that. These things we fix every three years in negotiations but always bearing in mind that we are partners." Shortly after that I entered into the TV/theatrical negotiations, and needless to say they went smoothly.

That was truly a blessing, not just for the union but for me personally. A short time after the commercials strike I was diagnosed with prostate cancer and had to undergo surgery.

For the TV/theatrical negotiations I insisted that we work closely with the WGA—the Writers Guild of America (which was about to have its own negotiations with the studios). When we compared our contracts with the WGA contracts we had a dramatic moment—it took two actors on our committee (David Jolliffe and George Coe) to realize that we had been losing millions of dollars each year due to an oversight. Producers had insisted that our contracts were the same as those of the writers, but David and George discovered that we were in fact not receiving the same amount for pension and health benefits.

And no thanks to the highly paid SAG staff—they never noticed the disparity even though it had existed for fifteen years.

On that triumphant note my two difficult years were over.

And here is where the story takes its darkest turn. Our political opposition in the union began a campaign of attacking—no, vilifying—anyone who had been associated with the strike. Even though New York actors had *unanimously* voted for the strike and actively participated in it, they were now saying that the whole thing was a mistake and began mercilessly launching ad hominem attacks via email. They unfairly named actors in these emails who had done nothing but give up their personal and professional lives to make the strike a success.

Although New York was making me out to be the chief villain—odd, considering the fact that I still considered myself a New York actor—I was able to take it. But I felt horrible for the strike captains and other actor-organizers who were now unfairly being depicted as fools and idiots.

It was important for our political enemies to paint the strike as a failure. If they gave us any credit, how could they possibly win the next election? And they were so successful in their strategy that they were able to win back the next presidency, with Melissa Gilbert defeating the immensely talented and qualified Valerie Harper, who lost no doubt because she was one of our biggest supporters. Melissa had run her campaign against Valerie by attacking what we had done over the last two years, promising that there would be no further strikes on her watch. Another player who entered the picture also made sure that there would be no "job action"—the new NED, whom we knew to be a former studio executive but who was also, unbeknown to us at the time, a board member at Netflix (as well as a large stockholder). At worst, the fox appeared to be in the henhouse. At best, his position was clearly a conflict of interest. This man, by the way, would later go on to head up the Motion Picture Association of America (MPAA), the chief lobbying group for the major studios.

By continually declaring that the commercials strike was a failure (and convincing the membership of this false premise), they have virtually ensured that the membership will never again approve a strike, and without the ability to strike, our union—any union—has no power whatsoever. They have effectively undermined every negotiation ever since. As a result, actors today are receiving residual checks that are in some cases literally in the amount of *one cent*. I'm not kidding. *One cent*. Actors have gotten only a tiny increase in residuals over the past fifteen years on made-for-cable TV shows, a billion-dollar industry. The Internet is essentially a residual-free zone except for high-budget scripted shows (where, even there, the residuals formula does not result in a living wage).

It's now almost impossible for the average working actor to make a living—*except in commercials*. Go figure.

Bonnie continued her union activism at SAG for a number of years after I left office. But for me, I was finished with all of it. The presidency was not something that I ever enjoyed. It wasn't something that made me feel important. I certainly didn't have any political ambitions. So for me it was simply a way to have payback time for all the luck and good fortune I'd had over the years while working under union contracts. I was able to stand up for the "little guy."

In the end I had a sense of accomplishment, but the whole thing left me with such ill feelings that I vowed never to enter the SAG building again. I broke that vow recently when I attended a memorial for union hero George Coe. I'm hoping—for several reasons—that it's the last time I ever have to go there.

On the other hand, during my presidency there was a sense of camaraderie that I hadn't felt since I was in the army. I was never in the trenches during World War II, but it certainly felt like that during my two years at the union. However, I got to know and respect some great people I never would have met had I decided on that fateful day in Art's Deli to say no.

17

Epilogue?

I've yet to finish the last chapter of my life, so this isn't actually an epilogue. It's just the last chapter of the book. As of this writing I am almost 90 years old, but I continue to work as an actor. (I'm still a baby compared to my friend Norman Lloyd, who, as I said, continues to work at the age of 102.) I've never considered retiring; in fact my motto has always been that "old actors don't retire—the phone just stops ringing." That hasn't happened yet, but there have been times when there was a long wait between calls.

During my presidency at SAG I put my acting career on hold. There have been other SAG presidents who didn't do that, but for me there was no other way to handle the enormous responsibility that had been put before me. When at long, dear last I was out of office, I hadn't worked for two solid years, something that hadn't happened to me since the 1950s. But when life hands you lemons—you travel.

Bonnie and I left with some friends and traveled in Greece and Turkey on private boats—not on tours, just lots of beautiful scenery and relaxation. I was in no hurry to get home and see if anyone was looking for me.

My first job when I got back in the game was an easy one—a pleasure. I did a guest spot on *Scrubs*, with me and Ed Begley Jr. playing doctors in an obvious tribute to our roles on *St. Elsewhere*.

For the next few years I did other guest spots—mostly small roles. I've never enjoyed doing small roles—but not for the reason you think. I've always felt that there is a lot more pressure on the small roles because they're "expositional"—they're in the script to move the plot along, and it's much harder to create a believable, interesting character in a small part than with a starring role. And a bad performance by a small supporting character can completely take the audience out of what might be a great film or series. It's much harder than it looks, and I've always had the utmost respect for actors who can come in and nail a role like that in just a couple of takes (which is what they're expected to do so that the camera can take its time concentrating on the stars).

In my inimitable fashion I turned down some things during this period, but there were some memorable moments with parts that I took for nostalgic (and in some cases monetary) reasons. An episode of *Touched by an Angel* reunited me with Bonnie as my onscreen wife and with director Peter Hunt from *1776*.

I did an episode of a show called *Lost at Home*, which reunited me with writer-producer Michael Jacobs. And then there was the reprise of my voice as KITT for several products and shows, including two episodes of *The Simpsons*—my son Robert's favorite show and the longest running scripted TV series in history. (I was also hired to do the voice of KITT on a navigational system for automobiles; I'm still asked to do the voice for commercials.)

My role on *The Closer* was not a small role, and it turned out to be a big challenge. It was an all-night shoot, starting in the evening and going until the wee hours of the next morning. And I had a lot of "walk-and-talk" dialogue, something I hadn't done in many years. But it turned out very well.

I did the film *Blades of Glory*, a very funny film with funny people Will Ferrell, Jon Heder, Will Arnett, and Amy Poehler. It was the first feature film I had done since the 1990s. Although I had done a number of well-known films earlier in my career, my TV work was even better known, and so Hollywood had come to think of me as a TV actor. There had long been a kind of rule in show business that if you're a TV actor you aren't allowed to be a film actor. With the ascension of HBO and other high-quality networks where the work is more like what you'd see in movie theaters, the line has become blurred, with stars going back and forth between the two mediums without any career consequences.

I also did something I'd never done before. All my work until now had come as a result of word of mouth. I'd never been actively involved in the promotion of my career—I never did any of things you're supposed to, like hire a publicist. I also had never asked to be cast in something, but I enjoyed *Boston Legal* and especially the work of James Spader, so I asked my agent to call the producers. They immediately offered me a role. I'm sorry to say it wasn't a happy experience. I played a judge who had very little to say and sat for hours—too many hours—on the bench listening to long speeches by the attorneys. For someone who used to be the one delivering those speeches, both on the stage and on camera, it was difficult.

I then entered a period of unemployment that was twice as long as the previous one. Although I was still in demand as a celebrity, with constant offers to appear at autograph shows or to do the voice of KITT—someone even offered me thousands of dollars to record his proposal of marriage to his girlfriend—for about four years I didn't work as an actor. But I got a chance to play my favorite role— lucky grandfather.

We don't know much about the birth parents of our two adopted sons, but when I told our son Rob that his biological father was Jewish, his response startled me. He said, "Now I know who I am." He wasn't kidding. Later Rob would marry a woman who was observant in the Jewish faith. They have two girls, Shaina and Eliza, and they live in New York City. Fortunately we kept our New York apartment for many years, and it was easy for us to go back and forth to New York and visit them (which we did frequently during my four-year "hiatus"). I still look forward to my visits with them even if it means having to abide by their wishes to eat at vegan restaurants.

My son Michael also has two children, Liam and Grace, whom we see much more frequently because they live near us in Studio City. With Michael's schedule as both a singer and a teacher, Bonnie and I have many days when we take care of the kids at our house. I enjoy feeding them and being their chauffeur, taking them to their various activities. I'm back in the domestic role I enjoyed with my sons. (A note about my being the chef at home: if I didn't do the shopping and cooking I wouldn't eat, but Bonnie takes care of all the bills and is my business manager, so we each have our duties clearly delineated.)

I mentioned before that my prejudice about adoption was unfounded. My two sons turned out to be extremely intelligent, and I'm always impressed with the fact that I can talk to them about practically any subject.

Just as Edward Albee had predicted in his note, "the bumbles" had turned into "very nice people."

And *their* children have proven to be smarter than all of us. I've had the pleasure and pride of helping them get the kind of education I wish I'd had (if you remember, as a kid, schooling was an afterthought between radio gigs). All four kids are artistic—they all draw. Shaina got a full scholarship at an art school but opted to study Japanese pop culture and photography at another college.

And they all sing, but I'm not pushing any of them into show business—I am no Papa Rose, to be sure—but I'm not discouraging them either. Grace is a natural soprano with a great ear and Liam is very funny and a very good actor, but I'm not sure that either one of them wants to pursue singing and acting professionally. Ironically, Eliza was accepted as a singer at LaGuardia High School of Performing Arts, once the High School of Music and Art, where I was a student so many years ago. It appears that she wants to be a doctor, however, like her mother. Perhaps they will all avoid the perils of show business.

I've said that the best roles I ever had were ones that fell into my lap, and that's exactly what happened with the character arc I did on *Grey's Anatomy*. If you've been reading this book—and I assume you have—then you won't be surprised that my association with the show began with the word *no*. During the show's first season Bonnie and I were offered roles, as a couple, that included a very dramatic death scene. I didn't want to do it—it wasn't for me. But Bonnie said yes and wound up having a delightful experience with George Coe as her onscreen husband.

Then in 2014 the producer of the show, Tony Phelan, asked to meet with me. I suggested Art's Deli (my informal office), and we had a pleasant conversation. Looking back on it, I think he was making sure that, at eighty-six, I still had all my marbles. Shonda Rhimes, the creator of *Grey's Anatomy*, has had an extraordinary career, with three network shows running at the same time ("Shonda Thursday" on ABC) and several more in development. Evidently she wanted me for the role of Dr. Craig Thomas. (I wondered if this character's name was a tribute to my role in *St. Elsewhere*, Dr. Mark *Craig*.)

Dr. Craig Thomas was an old-school surgeon (I could play that) who was brought in to be Sandra Oh's curmudgeonly mentor (I could play that, too). Dr. Thomas was always ready to bring Sandra's cocky character of Dr. Yang down a peg or two. Sandra and I had great chemistry, and our scenes were a pleasure—though they weren't all easy. Again I had to do those "walk-and-talk" scenes with lots of medical dialogue, something we'd pioneered on *St. Elsewhere*, but a couple of decades had passed since I'd been asked to do that. The producers were pleased, and I wound up guest-starring in five episodes. My character finally dies while standing next to an operating table. They hired a stuntman to literally "take the fall" since there was no way I was going to do that.

Funny story about the show—there was a young woman who kept following me around, offering me coffee, offering to help in any way possible. I was convinced that she had a crush on me. I got home and told Bonnie what I thought and she laughed. She informed me about something I should have already figured out—the young woman was a production assistant being paid specifically to take care of me. Talk about being brought down a peg or two.

That's the main thing that Bonnie and I have shared during our long, long marriage: laughs. It's now almost seventy years, and our situation is almost completely unique in the annals of Hollywood marriages: two successful actors, never married to anyone else, who remained together for the rest of their lives. The only other example I can think of is the late Eli Wallach and Anne Jackson.

And then there are a few examples of Hollywood marriages that have survived for decades but only after one of the partners quit the business to raise children. Bonnie slowed down a few times during her career to concentrate on the kids, but she never left the business.

I don't know if Bonnie and I are the only living actors in this rare situation, but it's quite an accomplishment and it's certainly something that I've come to appreciate more every year. How did we do it? Was it the therapy? Ironically, one of our therapists said that it was just karma.

Thanks to Michael Jacobs I've never had to worry about the word *debt*, and so I will forever be in *his* debt. I can honestly say that he is single-handedly responsible for the financial security I've enjoyed for several decades, so whenever he has asked me to do something, I'm there. He asked me to return to the role of Mr. Feeny for his reboot of *Boy Meets World*, called *Girl Meets World*, in which Cory and Topanga, the kids from the original show, now have a kid of their own, a daughter. I've recurred on the show for three seasons now.

I have no idea if this will prove to be my last job. I hope not—I still haven't fulfilled my lifelong dream of doing a western. I loved all those John Wayne/John Ford films, and although I won't get to work with either of them, maybe I'll still get a chance to do a western— maybe someday I'll play the town drunk or something.

The idea of working again actually makes me happy. It's only taken eighty-plus years to get to this point.

Reading over the first chapters of this book after I first wrote them drove me back into therapy. I was depressed thinking about my family, especially my sisters, who didn't enjoy the kind of life that I've led.

Dr. Shane said that it wasn't depression. She said, "I think you're in mourning for your lost childhood." My level of anxiety while reading these pages—some of which literally brought me to tears— finally convinced me of my psychologist's analysis: I was indeed an abused child. Why did my mother have to drag us around, throwing back carpets in her friends' apartments, demanding that we dance like trained monkeys? And why was I such a wimp and couldn't say no? In my defense, I was just a child. But still . . .

As a result I was constantly haunted by negative feelings when it came to performing, from almost the time I was born. I kept it all to myself when I was young, and so whatever followed, the nega- tivity poured out of me. The sharp, abrupt comments and retorts I was famous for in my roles were unfortunately part of my daily per- sonality. But is it possible to have a negative attitude, which is still a part of me, and at the same time a positive attitude, the part of me that is willing to admit who I am and what I've accomplished? Human beings have "self states" within us—two, or even more—

and we can move from one state to another. I've lived in a constant state of ambivalence my entire life, at least when it's come to acting.

It's only over the last couple of years—since I started writing this book, in fact—that I began to change and drop the barrier I'd set up. I'd always say to myself and others that I never wanted to be an actor—that I had been forced into it as a child. But I've come to realize this statement was only to protect myself over the years from any potential rejection and the fear of failure. I've continually said that acting was never my dream, that it was never my choice. However, in the few stages of my life when I had the chance to do something else, I never made the effort. When I first got out of the army, I could have gone to a college *without* a theater department. During my misery in the early New York years, Bonnie encouraged me to go back to school and study something I loved, like archaeology. Archaeologist? I didn't do it. Since the time that I was a little boy and to this very day, I love to stare up at the moon and the stars. I love reading about new discoveries involving galaxies and planets. Astronomer? I didn't do it.

Clearly acting is what I wanted to do and what I've always wanted to do in spite of the countless times I said no and tried to push it all away.

One time I was out getting a slice of pizza on Columbus Avenue with the eldest of my four grandchildren, Shaina (age eight at the time). We have over the years had some trouble making conversation, but there we were, dutifully sitting across the table from each other. I was trying to think of what I might say to break the silence when we were interrupted by a somewhat buxom lady and three of her kids, all babbling at once as they surrounded our table.

"We saw you! We watch every show! Mr. Feeny!"

By then the pizza had arrived and Shaina was totally focused on it. She didn't even look up.

"Yes, yes, that's me, Mr. Feeny," I said, nodding and smiling.

The appreciative family finally left, and Shaina, still without looking up from her pizza, said in complete deadpan, "What was *that* all about?"

I was thinking the same thing.

Celebrity has always been a little like that for me. I talked about the fact that I never learned to bow. Didn't I enjoy the applause, the audience's approval? Part of me must have enjoyed it, but another large part was saying, "Okay, that's done. You all seemed to have enjoyed yourselves. Now I want to go home."

There was none of that basking in the waves of applause that some actors seem to enjoy so much. I mention this because I feel I've robbed myself of something I might have savored and enjoyed. After all, isn't that why someone becomes an actor? To enjoy the recognition, the applause, the laugh? But then again, it wasn't my chosen profession. Or so I kept telling myself.

I'm finally at the point where I'm ready to proclaim it: I am an actor—a very good actor—and I am happy to know that I wound up where I evidently belonged. There's something to be said for the recognition that comes with a job well done—and I'll take it.

Frances Fisher, a terrific actress and longtime fellow warrior as a SAG board member, put together a surprise party for my eightieth birthday. I was very touched, and I spent an incredible evening with many of the friends and colleagues who had been part of the SAG saga some four or five years earlier. That was the only time I'd really been part of a tribute, and I'm glad it was a surprise party because if they'd asked in advance I would have said no (and I'm sure they knew that).

But that was almost ten years ago and I've changed. When the Turner Classic Film Festival invited me to another tribute—the premiere screening of the Blu-ray release of 1776—I didn't want to go, but when I learned that I wouldn't have to give a speech, I agreed. As for dealing with the applause? I can honestly say that I enjoyed the standing ovation as I came onto the dais, and the Q&A that followed with TCM host Ben Mankiewicz was a lot of fun.

A performance of 1776 was recently presented as part of the Encores! series at New York City Center, and a conversation between Lin-Manuel Miranda and myself was published in the program notes (see the appendix of this book for the text of the conversation). Lin-Manuel, who is the genius behind Hamilton, told me he was a fan of Mr. Feeny. We also discussed how 1776 paved the way for his own show about the founding fathers of our country. As for me, I'm very inspired by the excitement this Renaissance man and his work have created once again in musicals. As he said in the interview, "Musical theater, when all the elements are clicking, takes us to emotional places nothing else can touch."

For my eighty-ninth birthday I traveled to New York, where I was a guest at performances of both *1776* and *Hamilton*.

Over the years I've frequently been asked if I have advice for young actors. And here's what I've always said: *Don't do it.*

I may still say that but only to get a laugh.

All those years ago, back when I was doing *Life with Father*, Howard Lindsay taught me to never let a laugh run its full course.

"Leave them wanting more," he said.

So, with a nod to Mr. Lindsay, I'll stop right here.

APPENDIX

The Legacy of *1776*: A Conversation with
William Daniels and Lin-Manuel Miranda

Matt Weinstock edits the publications at New York City Center and participated in this interview, which is condensed and edited here and is reprinted courtesy of Playbill. *Grateful thanks to Bonnie Bartlett, Sharon Ellman, and Owen Panettieri for making this conversation possible.*

This spring, Encores! is reviving *1776*, Sherman Edwards and Peter Stone's irresistible Tony Award–winning musical about how the founding fathers signed the Declaration of Independence and gave birth to a new nation. To celebrate its return to New York, we brought together two extraordinary men of the theater—both of whom have logged a lot of hours in Revolutionary-era frock coats. William Daniels played John Adams in the original Broadway production of *1776*, and Lin-Manuel Miranda wrote and stars in the Broadway juggernaut *Hamilton*. In a recent phone call, Daniels and Miranda traded thoughts on why *1776* works so brilliantly, how the musical helped shape *Hamilton*, and what it's like to perform for a sitting U.S. president.

LIN-MANUEL MIRANDA: Mr. Daniels, I'm talking to you from the lip of the stage of the Forty-Sixth Street Theatre—

WILLIAM DANIELS: *(laughs)* Oh, my god.

LM: —where you did *1776*, and where we're doing *Hamilton*. It's now the Richard Rodgers. My first question is: Which dressing room was yours? Were you stage right?

WD: I think I was. Stage right, with a little door facing the audience.

LM: You either [had] our stage manager's office or you [had] George Washington's current dressing room.

WD: *(laughs)* How are you holding up, doing eight a week?

LM: It's a lot. But, you know . . . it's all my *fault*. I really have no right to complain. I wrote the words that I say, and I gave myself a lot of them.

WD: Well, I would much prefer to have met you personally, rather than over the phone, and shake your hand for the great success you've had with *Hamilton*.

LM: Thank you, sir. Likewise.

WD: I really am looking forward to seeing it. We're planning to go back to New York soon. I know it's a very tough ticket to get—but I'll give it a try.

LM: I know a guy. I'll make it happen.

WD: *(laughs)* That's very good. And I want to pay for them, for sure. I'm sure the producers keep a sharp eye on the weekly gross.

CITY CENTER: Before we get too deeply into ticketing, I want to talk a bit about *1776*. Today we think of it as being in the pantheon of great musicals, but in the 1960s the show was so unconventional that Sherman Edwards had a hard time getting it produced. "Some of the biggest [names] in the theater," he recalled, "looked at me and said, 'What, a costume musical? A costume, historical musi-cal?'" Mr. Daniels, do you remember your initial reaction to the idea?

WD: I read the script with a bunch of people at somebody's apart-ment. Sherman Edwards was a former schoolteacher from New Jersey, and he had written not just the songs, but the script. It was a little stiff; I remember thinking, *We're in the middle of Vietnam, for Christ's sake, and they're waving the flag?* I really had to be talked into doing it. At any rate, when the script came back to me, Peter Stone had taken ahold of it, and he'd gone back to the actual con-versations in the Second Continental Congress. He had written them out on little cards and injected them into the script, and it made all the difference in the world. It added humor and concise-ness and truth.

LM: I love that anecdote, because it gets at something that I discovered in writing *Hamilton*: the truth is invariably more interesting than anything a writer could make up. That Peter Stone went back to the texts written by these guys, who were petty, brilliant, compromised—that's more interesting than any marble saints or plaster heroes you can create. And the picture you all painted together of John Adams was so powerful; in the opening scene, he calls himself "obnoxious and disliked," which is a real quote. We don't have a John Adams in our show, but we can just refer to him, and everyone just pictures *you*, Mr. Daniels.

WD: Really?

LM: Yeah. *1776* created such an iconic, indelible image of Adams that we just know who that is now. It's also, I think, one of the best books—if not *the* best—ever written for musical theater, in that you *long* to see them talk to each other. Which almost never happens in a musical. Most musicals, you're waiting for the next song to start. That book is so smart, and so engaging.

WD: Howard Da Silva played Ben Franklin, and he said to me, "Bill, we've *got an ending.*" *(laughs)* And we did; we always had that rousing stage picture of them all standing there and signing the Declaration of Independence.

CC: How did you discover *1776*, Lin-Manuel?

LM: I came pretty late to *1776*—probably college. I fell in love with the movie, and it's a singular movie because it has that incredible original cast doing their thing. That's very rare. Can you talk a little bit about that opportunity?

WD: That was Jack Warner. He saw the show and said, "I want the whole cast."

LM: That was amazing.

WD: I think it was a cheap way to go. Also, he felt he had made a mistake using Audrey Hepburn in *My Fair Lady* instead of sticking with Julie Andrews.

LM: *Wow.*

WD: He didn't want to make that mistake again, so he hired the entire cast—and Peter Hunt, the director. I was disappointed in the film, because on a proscenium stage, the play had a certain style—and film is very realistic. And yet it worked, and people watch it. Every year on July Fourth I get all these letters saying, "You've made us look at history in a different way." As a matter of fact, doing the show got *me* interested in history. I think that may be the connection with your show, Lin-Manuel. I can't think of a musical about American history coming before *1776*.

LM: I'll tell you, I think you're absolutely right. *1776* certainly paved the way for *Hamilton*—not just in that it's about our founders but also in that it engages fully with their humanity. I think it makes them accessible to us in a very real way. To begin an opening number with everyone telling another guy to shut up—what better way to pull these people that we see on statues and on our currency off of the pedestal? It's an extraordinary opening number.

WD: That was always an interesting moment. Doing John Adams was one of the highlights of my acting career: you come out in front of the curtain, and the people are sitting there rustling their papers, and the men are probably wondering why they bought these tickets—and then you start, "By God, I have had this Congress!" And it was always "Con-*gress*." Sherman Edwards said, "You have to say Con-*gress*." That whole speech was done in front of the curtain, and then the curtain opened up and this whole choir of voices sang, "Sit down, John!" That really grabbed them. You know, Lin-Manuel, I saw the *60 Minutes* piece about *Hamilton*, and I was so impressed. The way you put his story into music, into—I don't know what you call it. Bebop? Rap? It really grabs people. And it *has* to grab people. Otherwise it could be kind of boring just to talk about history.

LM: Someone said something really smart once: "You kind of have to work hard to make this story boring." My arc in learning about all this was actually similar to yours, Mr. Daniels, in that I didn't know anything about this era of history until I started writing it. And as I fell in love with the research, and these stories, I found that if you make the political personal, you can get away with putting in as much information as you want—as long as it *always* has a personal angle, and they remain flesh-and-blood creatures. Once everyone starts spouting, then you're dead in the water.

CC: Abigail Adams wasn't in Philadelphia during the events of *1776*, but she shows up in the musical as an apparition. Did the writers insert her to humanize John Adams?

WD: Well, Abigail was such a strong influence in his life, so it was important that she be in the show. I think it broke up the run of scenes in the Congress that we were able to get that song, "Yours, Yours, Yours," in there.

CC: And that song is largely made up of direct quotes from John and Abigail Adams' correspondence. Adams really did send his wife a "Catalogue of your Faults," and the song's refrain—"I am as I ever was, and ever shall be, yours, yours, yours"—came from a letter he wrote her in 1780.

WD: I've read those letters, and they're very moving.

LM: One of the great legacies of John Adams is his correspondence with his wife, because through that correspondence, we get to see the human side of all of the founding fathers. He describes Hamilton as "the bastard brat of a Scotch peddler," which is the line I riff off in the opening number of our show. During his time with Ben Franklin in Paris, he writes letters home to Abigail, being like, "I don't know what I'm *doing* here." In his frankness in his letters to her, we get to see the founders as people. And that's an invaluable legacy, because all of these guys had one eye on the prize and the other eye on posterity. They're all angling to look good, because they know they're going to be talked about. In those letters, you've got Adams being like, "Well, Washington's kind of boring." *(laughs)* He paints a very human side, because he's kvetching to his wife.

WD: Adams was known for never really feeling that he had said enough. You couldn't shut him up, you know.

LM: Well, there's a virtue in that. There's a virtue in speaking up for what's right. Adams and Hamilton were sort of the loudmouths of the founding fathers. *(laughs)* So it's nice that they've spoken up and had their moments in *1776* and *Hamilton*, respectively.

CC: Like *Hamilton, 1776* became something of a lightning rod for politicians. Vice President Hubert Humphrey said, "This is how history ought to be taught," and in February 1970 President Nixon invited the show to play the White House—making it the first full-scale Broadway musical ever to do so. What do you remember about that night?

WD: It was a negotiation that took over a year, actually, because the Nixon administration wanted us to cut "Cool, Cool, Conservative [Considerate] Men."

CC: Why?

WD: Because it was about *them.* *(laughs)* But our producer Stuart Ostrow said, "We won't do the show without doing 'Cool, Cool, Conservative [*sic*] Men.'" Finally they allowed us to do the whole thing. But when Stuart called and said they'd asked us to come to the White House, I said, "For *Nixon?!* You must be out of your *mind.*" Most of the cast were Democrats and felt the same way. There were about three Republicans. At any rate, we did go, and performed in the East Room. There was no room for the orchestra, so they were out in the hall, and they were playing too loud.

CC: The United States Marine Band was part of the orchestra that night, which might explain the volume. After the show, Nixon got onstage and spoke, didn't he?

WD: He stood next to Howard Da Silva and me. I think he inadvertently made an amusing remark, and when he got a laugh, then you couldn't stop him. It was a very memorable experience being there. Practically all of the Senate and the House came to see it, and at the end, they stood up and raved and carried on. It reminded me of that saying—"Patriotism is the final refuge of a scoundrel." *(laughs)*

CC: Lin-Manuel, you've said that you hold a ten-dollar bill differently now because "that's your dude." Mr. Daniels, did starring in *1776* change your view of John Adams? Had you studied him in school?

WD: *(pause)* To be honest, I did not have a proper education. I was working. I was in *Life with Father* on Broadway, and my sister and I were a song-and-dance team that worked at night. I went to a performers' school, with all the kids who were in shows, but it was run out of somebody's apartment and there was nothing going on there. I was never in class; I'd go in, say I had an appointment, and then go and read the *New York Times*. *(laughs)* Somehow I decided that I wanted to go to Northwestern University, and they sent the fellow who ran my school a questionnaire about my grades. He called and said, "Bill, you're applying to *college*?" I said, "Yes, yes, I am." He said, "I have this form here about your grades—but, you know, we had a fire here, and all my records are lost. Do you remember any of your grades?" A light went on in my head. I said, "Yeah, I think I do." *(laughs)* We went down the whole list and made up a whole bunch of numbers. I'd never had American history, and I gave myself an 88.

CC: Just an 88?

WD: *(laughs)* I didn't get greedy.

CC: Does it ever feel ironic, then, that an entire generation knows and loves you for playing a teacher on *Boy Meets World*?

WD: Mr. Feeny? I never thought about the irony of it.

LM: Listen, if we start talking about Mr. Feeny, we're gonna be on the phone another hour. *(laughs)* Because I am the same age as Ben Savage, and you helped raise me too, sir. But that's a conversation for another day. We'll have that in person.

CC: One last question: Stephen Sondheim has said of you, "Lin knows where musical theater comes from, and he cares about where it comes from." Why is that sense of history important? What do we lose if we stop performing, and listening to, great musicals from the past?

LM: Well, the answer is simple—you learn from what inspires you. Musical theater, when all the elements are clicking, takes us to emotional places nothing else can touch. It's very tricky to get right. Why would you not want to learn from the ones that got you there?